Pirate Ghosts & Phantom Ships
Thomas D'Agostino
Photography by Arlene Nicholson

4880 Lower Valley Road Atglen Pennsylvania 19310

Dedication

This book is dedicated to all who have lost their lives at sea. May they have eternal peace.

Designed by John P. Cheek
Cover design by Bruce Waters
Type set in Decaying/NewBskvll BT

ISBN: 978-0-7643-2744-5
Printed in China

Published by Schiffer Publishing Ltd.
4880 Lower Valley Road
Atglen, PA 19310
Phone: (610) 593-1777; Fax: (610) 593-2002
E-mail: Info@schifferbooks.com

For the largest selection of fine reference books on this and related subjects, please visit our web site at www.schifferbooks.com. We are always looking for people to write books on new and related subjects. If you have an idea for a book please contact us at the above address.

This book may be purchased from the publisher.
Include $3.95 for shipping.
Please try your bookstore first.
You may write for a free catalog.

In Europe, Schiffer books are distributed by
Bushwood Books
6 Marksbury Ave.
Kew Gardens
Surrey TW9 4JF England
Phone: 44 (0) 20 8392-8585; Fax: 44 (0) 20 8392-9876
E-mail: info@bushwoodbooks.co.uk
Website: www.bushwoodbooks.co.uk
Free postage in the U.K., Europe; air mail at cost.

Contents

Acknowledgements

I want to start by thanking my wife, Arlene, who not only took the pictures for this book, but also helped me to acquire the stories. I also must thank Dinah Roseberry for her dedicated help and editing talents

I would like to give special thanks to my best friends Rocco Desimone who is an expert on pirate history, and Kevin Fay who advised me on maritime facts and data. Matt Moniz and the rest of the gang at Spooky South-coast WBSM 1420 AM radio, Christopher Balzano of www.masscrossroads.com, Jeff Belanger of www.ghost-village.com, The Rose Island Lighthouse Foundation, Colonial Lantern Tours of Plymouth for their great information on the harbor, the Isles of Shoals Steam-ship Company, Ron Kolek Jr., Glocester Light Infantry, Dan Small, park ranger at Lynn Woods, Author and writer Mary Roach, Author Eleyne Austin Sharp, Kat and John McNiff, Ghosts of Newport Tours, Matthew Evangelista of the Pirate Museum in Salem, Ted Von Mechow, everybody at the Crow's Nest Hotel and Tavern in Gloucester, Massachusetts, the friendly staff at Mystic Seaport, the Salem Maritime Museum, and all the other people who did not want their names mentioned but their stories told.

Introduction

Upon standing at the Fishermen's Memorial in Gloucester, Massachusetts, Arlene and I realized that this book was not only going to be about ghosts. It would also serve to pay homage to the countless brave souls who have lost their lives to the sea over the centuries. It is truly an honor to present this writing for all to experience. From every port in the world, past and present, to all who have journeyed safely among the oceans, to those who have bravely met their maker. These stories and legends reflect the illustrious history of humankind's challenge with the sea. It also shows that what the sea has taken, cannot always be completely claimed.

Arlene and I spent two days in Gloucester, Massachusetts. Gloucester was one of the largest fishing ports in the world. It still retains a major status in such a role. It is also abound with legend and history that puts it beyond most seaside towns. We stayed at the Crow's Nest Hotel and Tavern. The Crow's Nest gained distinction from the movie, *The Perfect Storm*. The storm did take place in 1991 and the names of those lost have been immortalized on a plaque among the five thousand plus other names of Gloucester fishermen who saw no fear in performing their duty.

The people of Gloucester are exceedingly friendly. The Crow's Nest is a delightful place to stay for either the night or just a spirit or two. We were welcomed by all and became instant friends. Unlike the usual stereotypes, the people of this fishing community were friendly, helpful, courteous, and well versed in knowledge. They were tough as well but their kindness shone bright. We learned much of the wonders and tragedy these great people endure.

It is no wonder we find so much mystery in the oceans. There is much of the past still floating out there, just over the horizon awaiting return to a port that is neither in the present, nor soon to be. They are of a past moment suspended in time. These ghostly remnants of the sea, whether they are passengers of an ill-fated vessel, fishermen, or pirates, have yet to reach the peaceful vistas of their homes they eternally seek. Perhaps someday they will. Until then, maybe you might spy the countenance of a buccaneer, or witness the spectral glow of an unfortunate ship in the distance. If not on the water, then at least in your mind as you peruse these accounts that defy time and reason.

New Haven's Spectral Ship

Ghost ships are a strange phenomena, indeed. Those who witness the phantom vessels are forever changed by the moments the barks of the other world exude upon their once rational senses. In New Haven, the story is still recanted by old salts in the pubs. It echoes softly in the dark corners of homes that are dimly lit during the small hours of the night. This legacy has cast a mystical shroud that cloaks the seaside city to this very day.

The year was 1647. New Haven had suffered great losses trying to expand their colonization southward. They figured that by having ports in the Carolinas, they could increase profits from shipping. The Dutch settlers of the area thought otherwise and drove them out. Their shipping trade needed to move eastward. They looked towards England and acquired a one hundred and fifty ton vessel called *Fellowship*.

The great ship, built in Rhode Island, sat in port awaiting departure. It was loaded with the finest cargo of grains, lumber, precious furs, and some of New Haven's most cherished gentile. Captain Lamberton thought the boat was way too cranky to travel such a distance. He cursed it stating that it would be the death of them on the high seas. None-the-less, it was set to sail. Unfortunately, the icy breathe of winter blew heavily down upon the harbor, freezing it to the marrow. The *Fellowship* sat frozen at dock until the colonists brought ice cutters to the harbor. At once, they commenced cutting a path in the floes that gripped their last resort at bringing commerce back to New Haven.

Once a sluiceway of sufficient girth was cut, the ship had to be dragged out keel first. Having to be dragged stern foremost was irrefutably an omen of foreboding tide, thought the captain. Yet, the ship set its course and the journey began. The locals cheered as the ship railed along the ice path. They followed the boat as far as they could out into the harbor. Finally, it reached the end of the ice floes and started away. Reverend Davenport stood among the whooping throng as they offered cheers and prayers for the sojourners. When asked to lead them in a prayer, he rattled out, "Lord, if it be thy pleasure to bury these our friends at the bottom of the sea, take them: they are thine. Save them."

Needless to say the words that relinquished from his lips left the crowd stunned and agape. Within moments of this prophetic oratory, the last of the gleaming sails vanished from the horizon. Loved ones could only hold to prayer and patience for a safe homecoming. As the intensity of summer rolled in, the villagers awaited their kin's return. Many vessels came from England to the Port of New Haven but news of the great ship was nil. Not a single solitary jack tar or merchant had any recollection of such a craft coming to any port in England. Yet, the citizens of New Haven held to their faith that the vessel was in the safe hands of God. It would return.

A whole year passed with no word as to the fate of the *Fellowship*. It was now summer again and a great thunderstorm kicked up out of nowhere. As the tempest abated, someone spotted a speck of glistening white on the horizon. There in the distance loomed a proud ship, rich with sail and colors flying in the ocean wind. Much excitement arose as the ship entered the mouth of the harbor.

Recounting what happened next, as a matter of recollection by Cotton Mather, puts this most supernatural occurrence in a more sincere tone, as he was the foremost pious man of his era. As the ship drew near, the enthused denizens noticed a single man standing on the quarterdeck. The entity held frozen in pose, pointing a sword towards the vast blue sea. They also beheld that the wind was blowing with inestimable force against the ship, yet the sails billowed outward with full gale as it sped at a furious clip, contrary to the current of air. The sea remained calm under the bow of the vessel. As it bore down on the wharf, there was not a single ripple in the great ship's wake as if the boat was floating above the water and not within.

All at once, the horrible vestiges they witnessed made them realize they were not observing their ship, but the ghastly countenance of its counterpart instead. The mummified silence of the crowd turned to terror and screams as the main mast broke apart and the sails, now torn and tattered, fell towards the sea. The mizzen mast and bowsprit followed in the same surreal manner. The rest of the spars and sails collapsed away from her deck in turn until the wretched hull lay in ruins before their eyes. In one silent moment, the hulk disappeared into the briny deep. An ominous cloud then descended from the heavens over the spot where the hull had careened to its watery grave. That too, in time, dissipated and the calm waters of the placid bay were all the petrified onlookers had left to gaze.

The settlement's brave sojourners had come back to deliver the final message of their fate. Reverend Davenport saw this omen as a revelation of what had happened at sea. Many great authors have quoted the words that beamed from the reverend's mouth at the sight of this horrific apparition. "This was the very mould of our ship and thus was her tragic end. That God had condescended for the quieting of their afflicted spirits, this extraordinary account of his sovereign disposal of those for whom so many fervent prayers were made continually."

And so it is destined to be narrated for all time, the return of the phantom ship of New Haven as an omen of ill-fate. To this very day, it is written and versed how the villagers witnessed, for but a fleeting moment, the ghostly return of their loved ones.

The Pirate Lee's Eternal Ride

As flagons of ale clank back down upon the long wooden planks in seaside taverns, where hardy wanton souls relish in the nectar within, a story is roused. It is a tale of a pirate who, long ago, sealed his fate and is now doomed to relive the moments he forever forged. This is eternal punishment for his dastardly deeds.

Block Island is a small islet off the coast of Rhode Island. The islanders know the story well. It is almost a second nature narrative sliding off the tongues of the natives along the atoll. It is divulged with such consistency that one would dare not challenge the validity from where it has been handed down. The pirate's name was Lee. He was among the lesser educated and relied upon the vestiges of the sea trade for his keep. This was not very prosperous as he was also short on manners and personality. What he found more suited to his persona was the work of a privateer.

Lee's ship was moored in a Spanish port when a Spanish woman, aware of his impending trip to America, sought passage. One look and he knew the woman was quite affluent. Her purse was plump with currency and her jewels ripe for the picking. He immediately succumbed to her needs. He even let her take her white steed aboard the vessel. To a privateer, this was a bounty from the heavens. He need not hoist onto a ship. His booty had willingly come to him. The ship set sail for the new world.

Once out of lands eye, Lee's men stabbed the servants in their sleep as Lee himself smashed through her cabin door. The woman, though alarmed, kept her composure enough to elude the captain and made for the rail of the boat. She then leapt over the side to avoid the eminent fate that would have befallen her. In a moment of anger, Lee quickly had the horse thrown over the side of the ship as well. As the boat sailed from the scene, the shrieks of the horse sent chills through his henchmen. Soon all was quiet and he took to liquor and gambling to suppress the incident. During an argument over the division of the ill-gotten gain, Lee stabbed one of his own men and threw him overboard.

It wasn't long before they found themselves off the shores of Block Island. There in the cloak of darkness, they brought their bounty to shore and stealthily buried it. They saved enough pittances to pay for the wrecker's silence and welcome. This afforded them to live peacefully among the islanders for a year. During this respite from plundering, word had leaked to the authorities of the buccaneer's whereabouts. Lee had his men cast full sail on the ship and send it to sea unmanned as to create a diversion for the seekers of justice. They were basically castaways on the island after that.

A year had passed and Lee was soaking up some libations with his men along the bluffs one night when over the dark horizon came a spot of light. Very minute at first, the spot grew larger by the second. Before long it was upon them in full view. It was their ship in flames bearing towards them at a furious clip. The startled freebooters stared in disbelief as the vessel came to a halt near the bluffs. A shimmering white horse came to shore and bolted up the ledge towards the frightened throng. The men shied frantically from the nightshade but Lee, being their brave leader, scoffed their feeble ranting of fear and mounted the stallion. At once the steed was gone, carrying the pirate captain across the cliffs to the highest peak until it stopped short of the edge.

The sea was quiet and Lee could see the glowing ship below him. On the ship he saw, to his horror, the faces of those he and his men had killed, looking back at him. They remained expressionless with eyes as black and wicked as a shark, glaring up at him. The sun slid over the horizon and the steed forthwith faded from underneath Lee. There on the cliffs, stood the lone pirate. The ship had faded away, and the other men had run in terror.

From that frightful moment on, the corsairs who accompanied him on every whim, made themselves scarce of his presence. Even they, who were a fearless motley bunch, did not want to share in the wretched curse that was about to unfold on the ill-fated captain. Destiny brought its cruel wrath upon Lee. Even the islanders stayed clear of his company. Not one seafarer would give him passage on their boat for fear of being dragged to the bottom of the sea with the cursed fellow. The diminishing spirit of the captain began to show, as he became a hollow, miserable counterfeit of his old self.

Broken and destitute, Lee wandered around the island a hermit and friendless until one year later, when the spectral ship returned in the same manner. The phantom horse rose from the clutching surf to take the pirate as passenger once again. Now longing for peace, Lee climbed onto the shimmering wraith and they sped off towards the bluff's edge. This time the horse raged ahead at a flaming pace, heeding not the rocky brim. The horse and rider became airborne over the awaiting craft as it glowed with full sail. Again, the glowing apparitions of those who met an untimely demise at his hand were on deck, staring at him with fiendish grins. All at once the macabre mare plunged into the deep as a final mortal scream of terror permeated the night air. The glowing ship slowly dissipated, and soon the stars were the only specs of light left to behold.

Captain Lee was once again reunited with his ship, but had a new crew of the ethereal form. Their duty was most likely to sail the captain to his eternal torture and punishment for his murderous deeds.

Dungeon Rock

Thomas Veal and Captain Harris were pirates. Hiram Marble was not. Both pirates by all accounts died in 1658. Mr. Marble died in 1868. The two parties still frequently conversed with each other. How is that possible you ask, as the dates flash an instant two hundred and ten year difference between them? Well, read on and absorb one of the strangest tales of pirates, ghosts, and buried treasure. I must now relate the saga of a place where the spirits of pirates roam. It is not on the high seas but in a place well secluded from the waters in Lynn, Massachusetts. As you bring your tallow closer to this tome, I am confident you will shudder at the events that unfold in front of you. Let us now retire to the place called Dungeon Rock.

In the eerie pith of the deep forest, there sits embedded into an immense boulder, a foreboding iron door fastened with great creaking hinges. As the unwitting spectator emerges from the gnarling branches of the ominous trees that cloak the rocky outcropping and its metallic spectacle, the entrance becomes a beckoning vision that draws all to it. At first out of curiosity, then there are the voices, emanations from the void, pleading the tourist to enter. Why is the door there and who beckons?

Sometime before the earthquake of 1658, a strange dark ship approached the mouth of the Saugus River where it lay anchor. The few that saw the vessel noticed it flew no flag and was painted black. It was obviously the bark of pirate caste. Chatter rose among the villagers but

The black iron door beckons the brave to enter Dungeon Rock Cave.

none dared approach the sinister boat. It was then noticed that a dory was hoisted to the water below with four people aboard and a large chest. The dory rowed up the river. Soon it was out of sight as the waning light of day took the last specs of view from the curious swarm.

That night, it was very dark so no one saw the ship retreat towards the great wide ocean. In the morning it was gone. There was a note on the door of the Saugus Iron Works (c. 1650 and still in existence) pertaining to the need for some shackles and digging tools. They were to be promptly forged and hid in an undisclosed location. In return, a hefty wage of silver would be left in its place. This request was granted. The ironsmiths brought their wares to the secret place for exchange. They also hid in the woods to watch and see who the mysterious band was. The next morning the merchandise was gone and the silver was found as promised. No one ever saw who the pirates were. They crept into the shadows of the night and made the exchange right under the noses of the men on guard. They soon disappeared as strangely as they arrived.

A few months passed and the pirates returned in the same manner. It is known that they made camp in a place that was advantageous for hiding and spying on the affairs at sea. It was also clear that they were on the run and hiding out from authorities. They built a cabin and dug a well. There was even a small garden for their meager means. This place still exists and is known as Pirate's Glen.

Word got around that there were brigands hiding in the woods of Lynn, and a British war ship that was look-ing for the piratical band, arrived to investigate. They surrounded the meadow and captured three of the buc-caneers. One account states that the three captured were Captain Harris and two Spanish women, Clorinda (or Clorina), and Arabel. Another account claims all three captured were men. Either way, they were shipped back to England and executed for their crimes at sea. Thomas Veal managed to escape the soldiers and flee into the woods to a cave where they had supposedly buried their treasure. The cave was desolate enough for him to evade the hangman's noose.

He now was a lone corsair living in the depths of the fissure. Occasionally, he would venture to town incognito to obtain supplies. It is said he made shoes to supplement his income, but if he had such a treasure, why would he tarry so for meager pittances? Soon that matter was of no real conjecture as Veal left Dungeon Rock to captain a shallop crewed with fourteen men. This new venture was short lived. He was accused of piracy by Captain Daniel Staunton of Pennsylvania. The New London Magistrate put a bounty on his head and the chase was on. It was in New London Harbor where Thomas Veal met with Captain John Prentice in a battle that ensued all the way to Boston Harbor. Both ships fired at each other straight up the coast. Veal then turned and sailed towards Great Brewster Island. From there he returned to Dungeon Rock for good.

After word got out of the great battle at sea, the Court tried to enlist men to hunt down Veal and his gang of rogues. No one enlisted. They offered the share of the plunder that Veal was known to have on his shallop. Forty men finally signed on and boarded the *Province Galley* in search of the buccaneer. They sailed out of Boston not knowing that Thomas Veal had sprouted land legs and was hiding back at Dungeon Rock. Needless to say, their hunt was unsuccessful.

It is written by historian Alonzo Lewis, in the records of Lynn, one day in 1658, the ground began to tremble. An earth-shattering rumble sent the soil asunder as waves of fear and panic overcame the populace. Deep in the woods, Thomas Veal was holed up in his hideaway when the earthquake struck. A man named Joel Dunn was reportedly in the area when the quake hit. He came upon Dungeon Rock and saw a faint light in the midst of the crevice. As he descended into the cave, he spied Veal working by the light of a pine knot. Veal became irate over the intrusion and grabbed Dunn by the throat. At that point, the first great tremor enveloped the area. Joel Dunn did not remember the rest of the moments that ensued, or how he managed to elude the siege of boulders that poured into the opening. He was later found stammering outside of the cavern. The earthquake shook the area of Lynn with such force that the mammoth granite deposit split in two as the cavern collapsed, sealing Thomas Veal and the treasure in his rocky tomb for eternity. Well, almost.

Word has it that a few attempts to find Veal and foremost, his treasure, failed. Various people tried to blast through the rocky edifice but were left disappointed and broken. Two hundred years later, Hiram Marble, a member of the Spiritualist Church in Charlton, Massachusetts came to Lynn on a message from the ghosts of Thomas Veal and Captain Harris. He claimed that the duo told him he would find buried treasure and the bones of the swashbuckler who hid it there. Marble even kept notes of his conversations with the spirits of Thomas Veal and Harris. He purchased five acres of woods and set up his home near the rock. He began to tunnel for the buried treasure. Work was slow and tedious at the rate of about one foot per month. They would blast the rocks then carry the refuse out and deposit the boulders on a nearby hill. His initial funds had depleted. He then resorted to bonds and tours of the cave. For a fee of twenty-five cents, one could walk the passageway and even read the notes written by the phantom freebooters to Mr. Marble. The cave became a museum of sorts. One such letter written by the hands of a medium from the pirate ghosts, said to be communicating to Hiram Marble, reads as such:

Mr. Marble wrote: "I wish Veal or Harris would tell what move to make next."

He then covered the statement with fifteen pieces of paper as not to reveal the writing to the medium. She needed but only to feel the top piece of parchment before writing the pirate's reply. Thomas Veal replied:

"Dear Charge, you solicit me or Captain Harris to advise you as to what to next do. Well, as Harris says he has always had the heft of the load on his shoulders, I will try and respond myself and let Harris rest. Ha! ha! Well, Marble, we must joke a bit; did we not, we should have the blues, as do you some of those rainy days when you see no living person at the rock, save your own dear ones. Not a sound do you hear, save the woodpecker and that little gray bird [Mr. Marbles pet canary], that sings all day long, more especially wet days, tittry, tittry, tittry. But, Marble, as Long [a deceased friend of Marble] says, don't be discouraged. We are doing as fast as we can. As to the course, you are in the right direction at present. You have one more curve to make before you take the course that leads to the cave. We have a reason for keeping you from entering the cave at once. Moses was by the Lord kept forty years in his circuitous route, ere he had sight of that land that flowed with milk and honey. God had his purpose in so doing, not withstanding he might have led Moses into the promise, in a very few days from the start. But no; God wanted to develop a truth, and no faster than the minds of the people were prepared to receive it. Cheer up, Marble, we are with you and doing all we can. Your guide,

TOM VEAL."

Thus, on the orders of the pirate ghosts, Marble made many strange turns in his quest to unearth the treasure below. As one walks the cave to this day, it is amazing how the tunnel twists and winds almost in hairpin turns at times. Many more such communications would follow as the determined Marble toiled at the whims of his spirit guides to the final riches that lay beneath the rocks.

Hiram died on November 10, 1868, and was succeeded by his son and digging partner, Edwin, who passed away in 1880. The Marble family is buried in their home of Charlton, Massachusetts, except for Edwin who requested to be buried right next to the rock. His unadorned boulder is marked in pink near the entrance to the cave. Both of them tunneled about two hundred feet zigzagging into the ground at the pirate's request, never to discover the whereabouts of Veal and his treasure.

Although they spent their entire life and fortune searching for the elusive booty in vain, they did have one dream realized. Hiram wanted the money for land that would become a public park for all to enjoy. That part inadvertently was fulfilled. Now scores of people enjoy the vistas of nature and take in a moment at the dungeon where the black iron door beckons the brave into the tunnel. It is usually open for visitors. There lurks more than just stone and darkness in the uncanny pit. Many have witnessed the misty figures of phantoms moving among the confines of Dungeon Rock. Some say it is Hiram Marble while others swear it is the ghost of Thomas Veal still watching over his hoard of silver and gold. They have even seen strange lights like corpse candles flickering near the rock. Upon inspection, witnesses find there is no one there to cause them. No one living anyway. If it is Veal, then perhaps he is looking for someone to take marble's place in releasing him and his treasure from the icy clutches of the earth.

Arlene and I, accompanied by our friend and fellow adventurer, Kevin Fay, visited the rock on a beautiful November day. Thanksgiving was only two days past but the weather gave more of an air of spring than late fall. We were quite excited to be venturing into the crevice of much legend and lore. Once we had traversed the steep stairs leading to the cave, we found ourselves face to face with the ominous but unassuming iron door. We illuminated our lights and headed down the precipitous wooden steps into the crevice. It was almost breathtaking as we maneuvered through the winding cavern towards the deep bowers of the earth. At the very end, the tunnel was flooded a bit but that did not stop us from taking some EVP recordings and photos of the cave's interior. We were not successful in getting a voice on tape but the pictures did look like their forms were among us. It was concluded that the images were tricks of poor lighting and not of pirate ghosts. Still, despite no ghosts or other such supernatural phenomena, our trek into the rock was certainly one for the record book.

A visit to the rock is a must. The trail to it is clearly marked and there are remnants of the Marble homestead around the hill. The large boulder to the right of the rock is where Edwin is presumably buried. The voices may have been silent that day but that does not mean they are gone forever. When you visit Dungeon Rock, listen to the wind but heed not the pleas and promises of fortune, for they are but words of a pirate's ghost trying to lure you into a dark eternity as well.

Looking down from the entrance of the ominous pirate's cave.

The Saugus Ironworks where the pirates placed the note on the door for the mysterious order. It is now a National Historic Landmark.

The Screeching Specter of Marblehead

Although she is not a pirate ghost directly, the Screeching Lady of Marblehead is a spectral result of the actions of cold-blooded corsairs. The core spirit of the story is presented here. The reader may have heard some versions that have small differences but they all have the same ending, an eternal haunt.

It is told that a great ship carrying a large array of wealthy populace came under the sights of the most ruthless of brigands. They boarded the vessel, killing one hundred and fifty of its passengers before robbing all their possessions. One Englishwoman wore a massive ring on her finger. The pirates could not remove the ring and sought to chop off her digit. She jumped overboard and swam to shore. The pirates followed and caught her on the beach. There, they brutally beat her and left her for dead. As she was being tortured, she cried out "Lord save me! Mercy! Oh Lord Jesus save me!" The locals around the cove kept hidden out of fear as the woman was brutally murdered and robbed. It is claimed that the men of the village were out to sea at the time, leaving only the woman and children behind to witness the horrible event that unfolded in their ears. The next day they went to the beach and took her lifeless body for burial.

Another account states that the pirates took her to shore. There, they raped and beat her. Once they had accomplished their heinous deeds, they took her to sea where they threw her over the side of their dory. The woman was still alive and clung to the edge of the boat. At that point, one of the freebooters took his cutlass and lopped off her hands. She, of course, shrieked the same aforementioned beseeching words before relinquishing to the deep. The locals found her washed onto shore the next morning and buried her on that spot of the beach. One more account discerns to the reader that the woman was actually the daughter of a sea captain. She was walking the beach when the pirates came to shore. Either way, the accounts gave rise to the most ghastly annual celebration of terror from beyond. It is the ethereal moment from the past that the Marblehead residents must suffer eternally.

For hundreds of years, the people of the so aptly named Screeching Woman Cove have had to endure the final shrieks of that fateful night. Every year on the anniversary of her death, the screams of desperation echo through the ocean breeze filling the nearby homes with the final words of a woman, forever tormenting the residents whose ancestral background turned the other way.

Nix's Mate

As the sun recaptures the sky glistening over Boston Harbor, a lonely monument stretches from the briny deep to greet it. Its intention is to warn mariners of the rocky reef it lay perched upon, yet many consider it a burial marker for those whose souls lie with the boulders, unseen beneath the pressing waves. It is the last vestige of an extinct isle where lay buried among its remains, the bones of many a corsair. Freebooters of the high seas, whose fate was sealed by the hangman's noose that hung portentously from a scaffold on the highest point of the rocky atoll. The misty spirits that still pervade the quarter, and a curse rendered from the lips of an innocent man, remain as the only other testaments to the existence of Nix's Mate.

It is believed that the island of Nix's Mate received its name from an incident in 1636 when Captain Nix set sail with his crew in that year. Once at sea, the captain was ruthless and unsympathetic with his band. Woe to those who stood beyond his favor, for he would flog them on the deck, or chain them in the hold as a message to all of his absolute authority. At one point, the crew had taken enough abuse and mutinied while the ship was docked near the island in Boston Harbor. A harbor watch heard some dreadful cries from the vessel and rowed out to investigate. There, they found the captain viciously murdered in his bunk. During interrogations, the scallywag crew pointed the finger at the first mate.

Their stories were close enough in detail to convict the naïve sailor and he was found guilty of murder on the high seas. Punishment for mutiny and murder was death by hanging, and so befell the fate of the first mate.

Forever swearing his innocence, he was rowed out to the little island where the hangman awaited. As the rope was slipped around his neck, he began to vehemently cry for true justice to be served upon the men that carried out the evil deed. The crowd that had gathered for the hanging was moved by his sincere convictions. They knew the scurvy brethren he was cohort with were guiltier than he. Still, the powers that ruled ordered the execution to prevail. Before he hung from the gallows he made his final plea, "God show that I am innocent! Let this island sink and prove to these people that I have never stained my hands with human blood!"

As his words trailed off into the void, so did the sound of the rope ringing taught and creaking to and fro from the scaffold. The Magistrate thought justice to be served but it was only beginning. Many more pirates would feel the wrath of the gallows on Nix's Mate. It was customary in those days to suspend the executed from chains at the gibbet near the entrance of the city as a warning to those visiting. It was a town's way of stating the intolerance of criminal discretion. Those who entered the Boston Harbor would pass by Nix's Mate and get a glimpse of the destiny that befell many a freebooter as the hardened flesh fell from their long forgotten bones. Soon the bones of those left on the gibbet would crumble themselves and fall below to join the pile of others, who heeded not the grisly warning of ill will. The island literally became a graveyard of pirate remains.

Slowly, the claws of white and water began to claim the boulders and bones. Though the hanging of pirates and rogues continued, it was evident that the isle was diminishing in size. At some point, it was noticed that all but the hill where the gibbet stood had mysteriously succumbed to the sea. Old timers remembered the cursed words that permeated the air on that fateful day when Nix's first mate went to the gallows. Before anyone could remember much more, the island vanished into the deep, and the curse was fulfilled. The curse and island of Nix's Mate would seal the fate of men, innocent or guilty, never more.

Now, only the cries of innocence and mercy pervade the air surrounding the monument where the small island once jutted from the sea. Are they the cries of pirates gone to the gallows, or the caws of a lonely gull? Row out to the marker and listen closely, or look into the deep where the bones of those who paid a dear price for their dealings lay, but do not rest in Davy Jones Locker along with both Nix's Mates.

The Wicked Ghost of Phillip Babb

Having ventured to the Isles of Shoals, I became overwhelmed by two factors. The first was that people actually settled on these rocky outcroppings, and the second was that my wife, Arlene, and I were there. Literary greats such as Nathaniel Hawthorne, John Greenleaf Whittier, and Celia Thaxter wrote about the magical atolls with the zest of a child standing in front of a gift laden tree on Christmas morning. As the boat rounded Smuttynose en route to Appledore, I was no less excited than they had been upon beholding the wondrous landmasses. Arlene and I also hoped to witness one of the many pirate ghosts and phantom ships that still frequent the shoals on misty nights, when the wind howls ominously and the fog blanket beckons their arrival.

There are nine islands in all. Some belong to Maine, and some to New Hampshire. The isles are about ten miles from Portsmouth Harbor. John Smith recorded discovering the isles in 1614. He named them Smythe's Islands but that would soon be changed as fishermen found the plentiful waters to be a lucrative career. As the islands were settled, the names were changed. It was not very long before the next wave of settlers would grace their beaches and coves. Those were the infamous pirates of the East Coast. Many a pirate found refuge in the small islands from the authorities. Shoalers were very welcoming to brigands, who paid them well for their protection. It is no wonder some of them settled down on the small isles. Getting there is not as hard as one might think. Leaving there seems to be a problem, as many residual spirits still roam the shores and coves looking for eternal peace and freedom from the unforgiving Isles of Shoals.

One such resident is the ghost of Phillip Babb. Phillip Babb lived on Appledore Island where he was constable, butcher, and innkeeper. He was said to be a retired pirate who chose the largest of the shoals for his home. Appledore is one half mile wide and long. In the early seventeenth century, Maine imposed a tax on the island and the autonomous islanders rebelled by dismantling their homes and rowing them to Star Island. After that, the island became its own sovereign body. The Babb family cemetery is still on Appledore.

Phillip Babb was born in England around 1634. He married and had children with his wife, Mary. Some claim he was Don Pedro of "Ocean Born Mary" fame but neither he, nor his son's mortality dates coincide with that legend. If he was a privateer, it was well before Mary Fulton was born. Nonetheless, he left a legacy of freebooting and phantom sightings that the Isles of Shoals shall forever be witness to.

It would be less than inference to say that Babb's manners were rudely fashioned and kindled much disgust in his fellow islanders. He was also said to be a wicked, loathsome man. After his trials and tribulations at sea, Babb settled down to a safer career on the Isles of Shoals. More than likely to avoid the noose his friends and fellow privateers could not escape. He was known to wear a heavy butcher's frock with a great knife sheathed on a thick belt. He lived on the south side of the island in a cottage near the cove that now bears his name. It is documented that he and another islander dug a massive hole near the cove. It is recorded that he either found treasure there or was digging up one of his previous ill gains. Whatever the case, the hole was filled in and no one ever saw what came out of it, save for the one neighbor who helped him in his toils.

Phillip Babb died on March 3, 1671, and was buried on Appledore but he has not rested. He still roams the cove guarding his treasure from trespassers and hunters. One night, an islander was emerging from his workshop when he spied a wild form running towards him. At first he thought it to be an unsavory jest by one of his close friends. As the figure drew within arms reach, the man saw the face of a corpse with hideous sunken eyes. The angry wraith then heaved the giant knife from his belt and brandished it in the frightened man's face. There was no moment too soon for the terrified Shoaler to flee to the safety of his home, barely touching the ground along the way.

Another dweller of the island saw a figure meandering about in the moonlight at Babb's Cove. He could not make out the form as anyone he knew from the island. He called out to the outline as to what they were doing. The dark shade began to approach the apprehensive islander. The man thought it odd that he heard no footsteps on the gravel path as the silhouette approached. He then recognized the incarnate as the form of Phillip Babb. He could see the black eye sockets and glowing butcher's frock reflecting in the gibbous moon. He shouted at the ghost who then made its way down the path before vanishing into the darkness in front of the petrified islander.

There are many more accounts of the pirate-turned-butcher phantom roaming the island in the dead of night. Many have encountered the heinous spirit who wields a ghostly knife in their faces. Apparently he was so wicked and despicable in life, he cannot seem to let his attributes rest in death. As for the treasure, the great storm of 1851 filled the hole completely. A Coast Guard house now sits where the treasure is supposedly still buried. Was it ever found, or was the house put there to safeguard the cache and let the tired, evil ghost of Phillip Babb rest? No one is saying anything about it and Babb's spirit is certainly not resting peacefully.

Appledore Island is home to the wretched ghost of Phillip Babb as well as a few others.

The Vengeful Phantom Dory

Although not exactly a ship of great proportions, this next account does fall into the category of phantom boats. The Isles of Shoals has many tales of ghosts and ghoulish vessels that emerge from the thick of the foggy nights. This one is no different except that the boat and its ghostly tenant still wander the shores in search of interminable revenge.

About one hundred years before this narrative, in the early 1900s, the Isles of Shoals were common stops for many of the Guinea boats that angled the waters. Guinea boats consisted of Portuguese and Italian fishermen who sailed up from Boston to reap the bounties of the isles plentiful waters. These vessels became a familiar sight bobbing and swaying in the ebb and flow of the tides that crashed along the rocky surfaces of the islands. They were accepted and welcomed, as the waters were rich for the taking.

One night a crew member of one particular boat savored a bit too much in liquid libations and rowed ashore to seek revelry. The drunken man spotted the wife of an island fisherman and began advancing toward her in a manner most sinister. He immediately accosted her but the woman would not give in. She fought off the sailor's brutal advances until he pulled out his knife and plunged it into her, killing her on the spot. He scurried back to his boat. The crew knew something had gone wrong by the demeanor and blood. They immediately shoved off to sea saying nothing to anyone of the ordeal they had discovered. The crews of the Guinea boats were a very close group. Each one protected the other at all costs.

In the meantime, the woman's body was discovered and the authorities came to investigate. While the long arm of the law prodded and poked around with little success, the fisherman returned to find his home in an uproar. There were officers and neighbors mulling around everywhere. It was well documented that he and his wife did not get along very well. He was prone to a heavy hand due to a violent and quick temper. This was enough proof for the constables, who had no other substantial evidence to work with of his guilt in the evil deed. The man was immediately placed under arrest.

While preparing to transport their prisoner back to the mainland, a raging tempest rose out of the north. Travel became impossible so the group held fast in the fisherman's cottage awaiting the storm to subside. In the full fury of the storm, the fisherman dove through the window out towards the beach. There he secured his familiar dory and made his escape into the squall. The police rushed towards the angry surf only to spy the misty figure vanishing amidst the fog and wind, into the great wide sea. He was never seen again, or so it seems.

Several months later, the same Guinea boat made port in the isles and began fishing once again. In the dead of the moonlit night, a thick fog overcame the region, blanketing it with an impenetrable shroud. Suddenly the sounds of the sea were shattered by a blood-curdling scream from below the deck of the craft. All aboard raced towards the agonizing shriek but were not prepared for what their eyes would behold. There on the floor, was their fellow crewmember lying in a pool of blood. His severed hand lie just inches from the stump of his wrist. They all knew he was the man who had enacted the ruthless crime on the island months before. During the melee, someone distinctly heard a set of oars lock into the tholepins of a dory, followed by the swishing of water as if someone was rowing into the thick of the night. Another crewmember swore that he saw a figure disappearing into the fog in a small boat. It appears the fisherman had returned to enact his revenge.

The phantom's appetite was not sated there. Every Guinea boat that harbored at the isles met the same fate. A sinister fog would roll in, soon followed by an unearthly scream as a poor innocent fisherman would be found hacked by a mysterious being. Some would have an ear lopped off or a foot, or even a hand. Some unfortunate sailor had his nose removed by the swipe of a large knife. Another poor lad screamed in the dark bowers of the haunting night as his eyes were torn from his sockets. Each time, the sound of oars could be heard echoing through the ominous fog. Sometimes the dark shade of a man in a dory would be observed vanishing into the murkiness.

Guinea boats appeared less and less as the phantom dory prayed upon them in regular succession. Soon the fishing vessels were like ghosts, themselves. They became a faded memory among the Shoalers. No Guinea boat crew dared transgress the curse laid upon them by their fellow crewmember on the baleful night. As for the phantom dory, it is still roaming close to the isles watching every ship that enters its domain. It would be wise to check your heritage before planning a lengthy stay at the Isle of Shoals. I certainly did. Vengeful spirits never rest, even when we have to.

The Pirate's Wife

Lunging Island where the lady ghost roams, guarding over buried treasure while eternally awaiting the return of her pirate husband.

One of the most famous told accounts of ghosts and pirates takes place on the Isles of Shoals. There are many recounts of the story. It is hard to wade through the swirling waves of legend to the calm pools of the truth. Beware all who set out to explore the tiny islands, for you will most certainly embark on a journey into the dark bowers of the spirit realm. The night has no sanctuary from the visitation of the ghostly lady in white that still awaits her loved one's return from the sea.

There are two camps of lore in regard to who the ghost really is. Therefore, there are two stories to tell. Both have the same ending. It is eternal haunting among the Isles of Shoals. The first version is of a pirate named Sandy Gordon who had buried a vast treasure on Appledore Island. He was a companion of the infamous Edward Teach who was better known as Blackbeard. Blackbeard liked him so much that he gave him his own ship, the *Flying Scot* to command. Gordon was a crewmember of the *Porpoise* when he met the captain's daughter, Martha Herring. Gordon was lashed onboard the ship by Captain John Herring when it was found he was attempting to court the young Miss Herring. This prompted Gordon to mutiny, take the ship, and eventually become marooned on an island near Scotland. From there he hailed a group of ships that happened to be led by the infamous Blackbeard. It is also written that they were marooned at the Isles of Shoals where Blackbeard was residing at the time. Either way, he became one of Blackbeard's best fighters. That is when he was awarded his own vessel. They took up residence at the Isles of Shoals where Gordon married Martha Herring. At the same time, Blackbeard married another woman he had aboard the *Queen Anne's Revenge*. Once settled on White Island, Gordon began the life of a married man. It is said he buried treasure there to maintain his retirement. This was short lived, however, as a British man of war came searching for the mutineer of the *Porpoise*. He sailed to fight and left his bride to watch over the treasure until his return. Out at sea, the British war ship overtook the *Flying Scot*. Gordon's ship was reportedly blown up in the battle and he never returned. Martha died on the island from the elements while waiting for her lawless love to come back. Some reports claim it is her ghost wandering the isles searching for her pirate husband.

The second and most told story is that of Blackbeard himself. Many pirates made the Isles of Shoals their safe haven. The islanders did not mind so much as they were paid quite handsomely for their hospitality. Blackbeard was one of the favorites on the islands. He was even married there in 1718. A brief island honeymoon followed and he was off to South Carolina. The term honeymoon might not really apply here. Honeymoon actually came from a ritual where a married couple would drink honey wine, or mead as it is called, from one full moon to the next. This was said to increase fertility in the two. Unlike Gordon, who settled on the islands with his wife, Blackbeard left his thirteenth wife (some say fifteenth) after their "honeymoon" on Smuttynose, to guard a vast treasure he had buried on Lunging Island.

Once in South Carolina, he reportedly met his friend's daughter and fell in love with her, bringing disaster and death in his wake of affection. He killed her suitor in order to have the woman as his next bride. His friend was very upset over his daughter's grief and ordered Blackbeard killed. Actual accounts say that the Governor of Virginia wanted his head due to looting of his ports. The Royal Navy set out and found him. A fierce struggle ensued but the pirate was no match for the captain of the ship and his men. He was shot and stabbed a total of twenty-five times before he fell to the deck. He was then decapitated and his head hung from the prow of a Royal Navy ship for all to see. This was after authorities had pardoned the hardened pirate for his evil deeds.

Meanwhile, his wife on Lunging was left to fend for herself. She died in 1735, after waiting fifteen years for him to return and is seen to this day wandering along the rocky shore reciting the words, "HE WILL COME BACK."

A man staying at the hotel on Star Island once roamed to Lunging Island where he saw a woman walking along the rocks. He was stunned by the fact that he could not hear the seashells crunching under her feet. He moved towards her and noticed she was not of this world. As he stood next to her he heard the words, "HE WILL COME BACK" emanate from her mouth. The same man would encounter her spirit again with the same eerie chant as before. He is not the only one to witness the specter. She has appeared since 1735 to scores of frightened witnesses.

There are reports of the same ghostly apparition on Appledore, as well as Star and White Islands. Records indicate that she bounced from island to island while living there, so it is entirely possible that she still roams the various landmasses the same as she did in life. Perhaps it is both the ghost of Martha Herring and Blackbeard's wife roaming the islands with the same eternal yearning. If you happen to venture to the Isles of Shoals and see a young woman in a flowing white dress, listen in the wind, for it might be the ill-fated wife of the notorious Blackbeard or the dashing Sandy Gordon ceaselessly watching the beach, and assuring all that they will come back.

Star Island and hotel where the woman's ghost is also seen. The hotel is reported haunted as well.

The ghost of a pirate's wife, presumably Martha Herring, is also seen on White Island. Numerous ghosts are said to occupy the rocky outcropping.

The Specter That Returned to Salem

Reverend Cotton Mather was the most respected clergyman of his time. In the latter half of the seventeenth century, the colonies were victims of massive attacks by demons and creatures of the lower dominion. At least this is what was perceived in his book, *Magnalia Christi Americana* where he speaks of these evils infiltrating the country with their ungodly wrath. The very course of his tome was to substantiate the cases during this time for future reference. These included cases of possession, witchery and demonic visitations, being of ally with the devil, and of course, the witness of ghosts and phantoms. The compilations of such an astute man must be regarded with some candor, even in a time when the fear of the unknown far outweighed the eminent dangers of the wild new world.

One such account concerns a ship out of Salem, Massachusetts. Captain Mark Walford resided in a small inn kept by a certain Deacon Hezekiah Peabody. The captain resembled more of an inhuman spectacle than not. His sunken eyes and bushy brows were only accents to his fanglike incisors that protruded from his upper lip. Even his burly seafarer's facial hair could not mask the portent appearance exuded by the mariner. Yet he was known to be a pious and respected sort. His Puritan garb was plain and his punctual advent at Sunday mass was uncanny. He was heard night after night pacing the floor of his quarters while his ship, *Noah's Dove*, was being fitted for sails and repaired for a long journey. The deacon did not tarry much over the late night clopping on the floors as the captain was always prompt with his rent, paid in Spanish doubloons.

Soon, the ship was ready and Captain Walford called everyone who was to sail aboard. It was a Friday and to mariners, that was a day of rest. Ill omen beset those who set sail on such day. The captain was undaunted by such foolish revelry and planned his departure nonetheless. Many had taken board on the ship bound for England to see their families. Two of the passengers were a young married couple of strange demeanor. No one had seen the likes of the two before. The man introduced he and his bride as Mr. And Mrs. Walter Severn, and nothing more. The relatives staying behind became apprehensive and thought that they might be minions of the devil, seeking to take their loved ones after they had reached the high sea. The farewell party turned into a foreboding plea of respite for the journey.

Upon entering the deck of the ship, Mrs. Severn took one glance at the captain and fainted on the spot. Her husband took her below as the crowd grew more tense with the incident. They also could not help but notice that the *Noah's Dove* was more than adequately equipped for defense against possible attack from pirates. With six guns, scores of muskets, and more than enough sabers, it seemed the ship itself was readying for the work of a privateer. The captain ordered the sails unfurled and at that moment, two more strange and nefarious looking men jumped aboard to aid in their departure. The flag was hoisted and the terror of the crowd intensified when, in the same instant, a great blackbird, like that of a raven landed on the hands of the town clock. The weight of the bird turned the clocks hands to a ten-minute asset. All these premonitions were too uncanny for coincidence. The terrified villagers bade their loved ones to abandon their mission but none would have it.

In a fleeting moment, a great gust of wind tore the ship from her moorings and cast her off to sea. The angst-ridden throng watched the *Noah's Dove* sail over the horizon and out of sight. It only took about ten minutes for the ship to disappear from the panicked eyes the people of Salem bore that day. As the day wore on, so did the wind, which began to pick up velocity into gale intensity. By morning the storm was a full tempest. The ocean's unforgiving wrath wreaked havoc on the shoreline and the clouds released their full fury of downpour upon the earth. The storm became known in history as the gale of 1676. Its ferocity was unmatched by any other. The petrified people of Salem attributed the hurricane to the strange passengers that took board on the *Noah's Dove*.

For three days and nights, the storm raged out of control, destroying everything in its path. Hail, fire, thunder, and lightening opposed the midsummer heat. Death and devastation were imminent. Surely, the *Noah's Dove*, as well as many other vessels, must have succumbed to such a squall. Finally the fourth day brought sun. The town rejoiced, yet knew they would never see their loved ones again. The sea calmed and the wind ceased to a blustery billow. The villagers looked out over the waters but knew they would see no evidence of the wrecked ship wash ashore.

Just as the sun abated, a shout was heard from the rocks above. Someone had spotted a ship on the earth's edge. The whole settlement was now in an anxious commotion. They rushed to the shore for a glimpse. Slowly a glowing spot appeared in the distance. It was coming towards Salem. A hardened old mariner was quick to point out that the winds were blowing away from the harbor yet the ship bore towards them at a steady pace. As she grew near, the townspeople could tell immediately that the ship was indeed, the *Noah's Dove*.

It was now dark, yet the ship glowed as if a bright light from the heavens had spotted her and was keeping her alit. The stars appeared in the sky but the ship, brighter than a bonfire, quenched their existence as it raced towards the docks. Reverend Zebedee Stebbin called upon the assembly to pray for the countenance, that they may find peace in heaven. Amidst the worship came the vessel, glowing like the coals of a blacksmith's furnace. The psalms were interrupted by the cries for help and mercy. Then the phantom boat itself began to melt before the astonished multitude. Many saw their loved ones on board disappear into the frightening screams and flames of the vision until it just vanished altogether. The night air was silent save for the gusts that carried the ghostly voices into eternity.

No one ever knew what exactly became of the *Noah's Dove* until many years later when an old man of good stature and character came to live among the people of Salem. He made friends but was mostly a recluse of sorts. On his deathbed he summoned the clergy and told them he was Walter Severn, the man who sailed on the ill-fated *Noah's Dove* many years before. While out at sea, the raging tempest brought an end to the ship when a bolt of lightening struck the masts and mercilessly burned the ship to the water's edge in the peculiar span of ten minute's time. He and his wife were the only survivors as they clung fast to a spar until they were sighted by another ship bound for Hispaniola. They arrived at port, and two months later sailed to England. His wife unfortunately took ill and died shortly after. He then sought passage to Salem where he could live out the rest of his life. The captain was indeed a pirate who once plundered the south coast. His wife immediately recognized him as the buccaneer who killed her father in the Gulf of Mexico. Although he had been a man of ill repute, he was determined to bring his passengers safely and honestly to their destination in England.

A ship sits in Salem Harbor where the *Noah's Dove* once returned to port from her watery grave. The harbor sits further out to sea than it did many years ago.

The Ghost Pirates of Goat Island

This next account is but briefly mentioned in many historical records. Even the history books about Goat Island and Gravelly Point in Newport give it but a scant few sentences. It is no wonder spirits roam the area. They are probably looking for a little more credit for their part in an illustrious history of the ports and island. Here is what I "dug up" on the subject of pirate ghosts. Make what you will of it.

So many pirates made Newport their base of operations in the late sixteenth and early seventeenth century that the London Board of Trade petitioned for help from the English Government. Every famous name in history knew the wharfs of Newport well. The people knew the buccaneers and received them with friendly, open arms. They spent freely and often paid a fine token for their anonymity. They were, do not forget, outlaws after all. Because of this constant unlawful activity, Newport became known as the scourge of the colonies. Privateers were sometimes greeted with processions from the whole town. It was truly a different time.

That was until the colonial leaders were forced to arrest the corsairs or face charges of piracy themselves. Things changed rather quickly along the docks of degradedness and in 1723, twenty-six pirates were arrested for crimes on the high seas. They were taken to Gravelly Point, an area across from Goat Island and hanged there on July 19, 1723.

From there, the executed buccaneers were taken to Goat Island (named after the fact that the colonists let their goats graze there away from the bustling ports) and buried between the high and low water mark. Now, when the sun gives up its domain on the earth, the fog horns from the nearby lights beckon the ghosts of those who swung from the gallows to come forth, and once again revel in the area they once called home in life.

In the dark of the misty night one can see the men rise from the water and ascend upon the shores of the island in search of those who brought an end to their illustrious careers. Harken not onto them, for you might be a descendant of the assembly who once welcomed them with open arms, then sent them to their eternal doom.

A storm battered view of Goat Island from Rose Island. Pirate ghosts are said to emerge from the surf in search of vengeance.

The Teazer Light

During the War of 1812, the American Government issued "Letters of Marque" to those who were adventurous. These letters allowed captains of ships to attack enemy vessels and plunder them. They could then keep some of the proceeds and turn the rest over to the government. This helped deter the enemy from U. S. waters and gave the government some funds at the same time. These privateers, as they were known, were prone to get out of control, attacking any and every ship they spied. That is when they were labeled as pirates and sought for hanging. Not all were drawn to the freebooters' side though. Lieutenant Frederick Johnson was among the honest. His eighty-ton schooner, *Teazer* was a remarkable vessel. It captured two ships, six other schooners, and six brigs of enemy colors in a little over three weeks at sea.

The *Teazer's* luck ran short when it was intercepted by the *MNS Domingo*. The schooner was burned and the crew was taken to Halifax where they were forced to swear under solemn oath that they would never take up arms against the king again. They were then sent back to America as regular citizens. But, as the saying goes, old habits die hard.

A new schooner, *Young Teazer* was built and commissioned with a Letter of Marque in May of 1813. The Commander of the new schooner was Captain William Dobson. Lieutenant Johnson served in her crew as second in command. They sailed from Portland, Maine on June 3, 1813 with the same mission as before. Although the *Young Teazer* had only five guns, (three were actually wooden dummies for weight and influence) the privateer roamed the Halifax Harbor wreaking havoc on enemy ships. She quickly captured five vessels and became the foremost enemy of the British fleet.

Captain Dobson was also a bit of an instigator. He would challenge ships many times his size to come and fight. Of course, they had other orders to stay put in the harbors. He gained the ire of the *HMS La Hogue*. The *La Hogue* was a double-decked seventy-four cannon man of war. While on patrol, the *La Hogue* spotted the *Young Teazer* and began to run it down. Pound for pound, and sail for sail, the chase was on. The schooner escaped the giant warship by tacking into St. Margaret's Bay but was spotted by the *Sir John Sherbrooke*, a Canadian privateer commanded by Captain Freeman.

Quickly thinking, Dobson flew a British flag upon his mast and the *Sir John Sherbrooke* turned from the chase. The *Young Teazer* headed for Halifax Harbor. Captain Freeman learned of the deception and angrily began a quest for the privateer. He soon spotted the *Young Teazer* and gave chase. A heavy blanket of fog enveloped the area. The *Young Teazer* was sure to elude capture a third time but when the fog lifted, the Canadian vessel was in sight of Dobson's schooner and bearing down on the American privateer.

Captain Dobson sailed into Lunenburg then past Tanook in an attempt to escape. All went well until he spotted the *La Hogue* dead ahead. He then sailed into Mahone Bay where he could hide among the many tiny islands before using sweeps to avert capture. The captain of the *La Hogue* intuitively sent out five large whaling boats with cannons mounted on their bows. They positioned themselves in a circular pattern around the *Young Teazer*. Captain Dobson knew there was no chance for escape. He told his crew of the eminent future they faced.

Lieutenant Johnson was aware that he would be hanged for piracy if captured after he had taken an oath to never again take arms against the British. He crept into the galley where he obtained a lantern. He then lit the lantern and threw it into the powder magazine of the ship. A tremendous explosion rocked the bay as the schooner blew into a million pieces. The light of the explosion was seen as far as Halifax and the Maine coast. Historical records say eight men survived the explosion while legends say all perished.

Since then, witnesses have seen a ball of light about the tiny islands of Mahone Bay. It begins as a small orb, and then grows into a massive wall of flames resembling that of a ship exploding in the dark of night. Then the light is gone and the shrills of the sea birds lay proof as the only other witnesses to the ghostly reenactment of a doomed privateer's last cling to liberty and dignity.

The Many Haunts of Captain Kidd

In regard to the volumes of information I have read on the life of William Kidd, I could fill a book myself. I will however, keep his life story brief and cut to the chase in keeping with the subject of this tome—the *afterlife* of the infamous Captain Kidd. It would appear that he is as busy a ghost as he was when his mortal frame roved the seas in search of plunder.

William Kidd was born in Scotland on January 22, 1645. The next records of his whereabouts turn up around 1689, when the British handed Kidd a "Letter of Marque" as a privateer in the Caribbean during the Nine Years War. He then helped the British during King William's War and settled in New York where he married a wealthy widow. This was not his settling point. He had become quite the privateer. Many knew him in legend as the brave pirate who plundered countless ships. He knew all the nooks and crannies along the coast and was well respected among his fellow freebooters.

The year was 1695, piracy was reaching a peak and New York Harbor was just one of the many coastal stops where ill-gainers spent freely in the revel of taverns and public houses. Government was very slack in keeping these rogues at bay. Lord Bellomont, Governor of New Hampshire, along with Massachusetts and New York, eventually hired William "Robert" Kidd to command the thirty-four gun, *Adventure Galley* in quest for raiding ships that endangered merchant trade. Sort of a pirate

Captain Kidd, along with countless other pirates, were first hung, then placed in a gibbet, as seen on left, where their bodies hung until their crumbling bones fell to the earth below. *Photograph by Arlene Nicholson courtesy of the Pirate Museum, Salem, Massachusetts.*

to raid pirates, if you will. He was also given license to raid French merchant ships as well. The deal was too good to pass up but the captain knew deep down something was amiss. He took his Bible and buried it on the shores of Plymouth Sound. He felt it too pious a book to accompany his devious projections.

This Bible is the talk of much legend to this very day. It is said he planned to reclaim his possession after retiring to a more virtuous life. Therefore, he took great precautions in its preservation against the earth's elements. It was probably buried in a small chest. The Bible was reported to have been gold covered and engraved with his moniker. Though the book has never been recovered, many witnesses who have traversed the shores of Plymouth have seen what appears to be a misty figure wandering the modern-day beaches. It seems to be in search of the right spot where something might lie deep under the sand in wait of recovery. Could it be the captain returning for his Bible?

Kidd sailed out of Plymouth in May of 1696. His first stop was New York where he expanded his eighty-man crew to one hundred and fifty-five. He then sailed south for provisions and plunder. Much to his dismay, there were no pirates to be found. While patrolling the waters off of Madagascar, his ship needed repairs and was soon off again. Somewhere between then and January of 1698, William Kidd went from privateer to full pirate. His marauding was out of control and warrants were put out for his arrest. Several crewmembers were listed as well. At this point, he had abandoned the *Adventure Galley* and took residence on a ship taken from the French East India Company called the *Quedah Merchant*. This, he renamed the *Adventure Prize* and sailed forth until the warrants were issued. To elude authorities, he grounded the vessel and transferred his possessions to the sloop, *Antonio*. He roamed the East Coast burying his loot at various places. He arrived in Boston in 1699. He buried a large share of his cache there and then filed through the streets with his men in an undaunted manner. Surely, he thought a man of his influence and friends would make him well in the eyes of the law. This was not the case. They were arrested on July 6, 1699, and spent almost a year in prison before being transferred to England where they were put on trial and convicted of piracy. Kidd was also tried for murder as he had killed a gunner named William Moor on his ship during an argument over the morality of his raids.

On May 8, 1700, William Kidd and a group of his cohorts were arraigned, tried, and sentenced to hang at Execution Dock. The trial lasted but one day. He was hung on May 23, 1701, along with some of his fellow crewmembers. They were then hung in chains at a distance apart from each other along the river where their decaying bodies remained for all to see as a warning for many years. Kidd himself was exhibited from the gibbet at Tilbury Point on the Lower Thames River estuary. The first attempt to hang the privateer ended in a broken rope, sending Kidd to the ground with a start. He was tied up again, and successfully executed. This is how William Kidd was known to have hung from the gallows twice.

Now, long after their demise, the captain and his phantom crew still watch over the hoards they protected in their perilous lifetime. There are many stories of the pirate lot coming back to ward off any adventure seekers or robbers of their eternal booty. A short distance from Northfield, Massachusetts is Clark's Island. It is said that the privateer-turned-corsair sailed to this secluded spot and brought to shore a very heavy iron chest. It was stuffed with riches of ill-gotten gain. After burrowing a deep hole, the great bounty was lowered into it. Then, as in pirate tradition, one of the crew was selected by lot and slain. His body was placed on top of the box of booty. Once buried with the treasure, his ghost would roam the vicinity, forever watching over the buried cache, protecting it from fortune seekers.

From time to time, when the dark of the night shrouds the land and the gales howl ominously, a phantom ship manned by a spectral crew is seen sailing upstream to the spot where the treasure was buried. At the command is a ghost with the familiar of the infamous Captain Kidd at the helm. The ship, then anchors, and a glowing dory is lowered by its side as the countenances of Kidd and four oarsmen move silently through the water to the island. The dreadful apparitions dismount the boat and greet the eternal watcher of the hidden hoard. When all is well, the ghastly wraiths reassemble in the demonic dinghy and row back to the main vessel. The radiant rig then embarks back into the void, vanishing among the wails of the wind and the spray of the sea.

Among the many places Kidd is said to have buried his loot, Hog Island is the most curious. Many have rowed out to the island, located just off the shore of Orleans, Massachusetts at Cape Cod, in search of the riches that supposedly hide under its crust. Needless to say, none have ever found any treasure or at least, never reported a claim. The cache is buried at Money Head on Hog Island. Those who are adventurous enough may gain favor from the ghost of Captain Kidd by holding out until the forthcoming seventh day of the seventh month. Then, and only then, if the moon is full, will the secret of the burial "X," be revealed by the watchful spirit of the pirate.

Of course there is one more task to prove your worthiness of the ancient coins. The following ritual must ensue: At the tolling of midnight, a sheep is sacrificed and the blood must flow freely from the wound. Where the trail stops at Money Head is where the treasure lies beneath. It is that gesture of sinister exploit that will gain esteem of the captain, where he will magically stop the blood over the treasure for you to dig. This obviously is a bit out of the law itself. When the captain was alive, such an act may have been common, but today one is subject to severe animal cruelty charges. It is not likely that this means of treasure hunting will go unnoticed as the perpetrator of such a deed is on an island and must row back to the mainland. The story probably goes back before metal detectors were in vogue. Although I must present this little piece of legend for thoroughness, I do not advise trying it. Lets let the good old metal detectors do the rest. Besides, they are a lot cheaper and easier to carry.

Another tale of Kidd's buried treasure and ghostly crew takes place in New Jersey. Captain Kidd knew he had to disperse his treasure. He harbored at Sandy Hook one dark night and proceeded to unload some of his ill gain with the help of his crew. The lawless lot, armed to the hilt, rowed boatloads of riches to shore and forthright vanished into the wooded area. Their stealth was uncanny. Well, almost, as two men were in the area when the dark ship dropped anchor. The piratical band could not see the witnesses in the moonless night. After the captain had buried a sufficient amount of wealth somewhere in those woods, the ship, *Adventure Galley,* Captain Kidd's prized raiding ship, hoisted anchor and sailed silently into the waning night.

The excited pair took to finding the vast wealth that was ripe for the taking. Not a coin turned up despite their tireless efforts. Soon they figured they could use help. They told their story around town and before long, the area was one great pit full of busy villagers burrowing away in hopes of becoming rich. Unfortunately, the captain was too wily for the townsfolk as no one ever uncovered a single piece of gold.

Many years passed and the wooded area became barren of trees and soon, treasure seekers. But not barren of the spirits that once traversed those grounds laden with trunks of jewels and coins. When the moon is new and the stars are the only torches the night provides, a dark misty ship comes sailing silently past and anchors along the shores of Sandy Hook. It is then that the phosphorous small boats, burdened with tattered crewmen from another dominion, slide over the side of the great ship and row to the site where they once landed centuries ago. The shady shades of the dead then carry trunks of a most ethereal appearance onto the beach where they begin their toils of burying them and celebrating in the most evil revelry. In an instant the devilish laughter and motley manifestations are gone and the ship is but a wisp trailing off into the ocean breeze. Many swear it is the *Adventure Galley* and its crew coming back to relive a moment in time. Others say it is the same ghostly crew pursuing the same livelihood on the other side as they did in their mortal frames. The treasure they supposedly buried at Sandy Point has never been found. Perhaps they feel that it is an incomparable safe haven for their pillage in both here and the after "pirate" life. Here are some other places where William Kidd's ghost has been seen.

Charles Island, near Milford, Connecticut was reported to have been visited by Captain Kidd. A few townspeople went to the island to dig for treasure. Suddenly, there was a heavy *thunk*. They uncovered an iron lid to a chest. The elation turned to horror when a shrieking, headless entity came flying towards the frightened throng. The figure descended into the hole as the treasure seekers ran in haste. When they returned, the hole was gone and the ground was unscathed.

The Isles of Shoals is another spot where Kidd is said to have left some of his plunder. Many ghosts are seen on the island and some think that his is among the watchers of the hidden hoards that are scattered among the atolls.

Not far from the Isles of Shoals is Kennebunk, Maine. Just off of Kennebunk is Damariscotta Island where the infamous buccaneer is, by tale, recounted to have toiled the salt pond there in hopes of hiding his wealth. He is said to have hung a chain across the large entrance to keep boats from entering where he dumped a portion of his loot. There are bolts in the rocks where buoys were reported to mark the spots of his treasures. Locals say the island is haunted beyond measure and therefore shy clear of the area.

One more interesting story I unearthed concerning the brigand Kidd was an account William Kidd told himself of a visitation by the countenance of his brother who was, at the time, living in India. The manifestation appeared in his ship's quarters and even reclined in his bunk before dissolving into oblivion. The fearless captain thought the incident to be a product of excessive grog, but when he touched the blankets, they were wet with the stench of the sea to accompany. Soon after, William Kidd received tragic news of his brother's untimely demise. The time of his brother's death occurred at the same moment he witnessed the sibling's wraith in his bunk.

Gardiner's Island is a place where Kidd's treasure was actually dug up. After Kidd's arrest, the Earl of Bellomont, Governor of New York, New Hampshire, and Massachusetts Bay Colonies found where the treasure was buried. This he had done by procuring Kidd's journal where the exact location of the stash was given. Due to the fact that the all monies found on the island belonged to the crown, he was forced to relinquish the booty. John Gardiner, owner of the island never saw a coin of it (supposedly) and brought the cache to Boston. The treasure was auctioned off in England to pay for the governor of London's Greenwich Hospital. There is no doubt that both the Earl and Gardiner helped themselves to a small token for their services. A small marker stands as a monument to where the fortune was recovered.

The Legend of Don Pedro and Ocean Born Mary

Although Mary Wallace was not exactly a pirate, this story is filled from beginning to end with buccaneers, bridal gowns, brides, big houses, booty, and of course, boos. The year is 1720. It is July 28 and the bow of the *Wolf* is pointed straight towards Boston Harbor. The ship is filled with Scottish-Irish immigrants headed towards Colonial America from Londonderry, Ireland to settle in Londonderry, New Hampshire on a land claim given to them by the Throne of Britain.

Off the portside of the vessel is another ship flying the flag of a privateer, or pirate, as we know them throughout history. The pirate ship bears down swiftly upon the *Wolf* and is boarded by a band of looters led by the ruthless yet handsome Don Pedro. As his men begin to loot and gather the passengers together, he hears a cry from down below. He halts his men and saunters into the hold with cutlass in hand only to find Elizabeth Fulton and her husband, James, tending to a newborn baby. As she holds the baby protectively in her arms the pirate sheaths his cutlass and asks, "What is the baby's name?"

"She hasn't one yet." The mother replies.

Don Pedro becomes quite overcome by the little new born baby and speaks with a more amorous tone. "If you would be so kind as to name the baby Mary after my mother then I shall see that everybody onboard this ship is returned their goods and left unharmed."

This is so done as the pirate himself crudely baptizes the baby in the name of his beloved mother.

The fearsome pirate exits the hold and returns a few moments later with a beautiful piece of green brocaded silk from the Orient. "This is for Mary." He says. "Use it for her wedding dress."

The *Wolf* made port in Boston and unfortunately James Fulton died shortly after. Mrs. Fulton took Mary and moved to Londonderry as planned where Mary grew up to be a tall beautiful red-headed young woman. In 1742, Mary married James Wallace and as requested did wear a gown made from the silk that Don Pedro bestowed upon her parents years before. Remnants of the famous dress are on display to this day at the New Hampshire Historical Society in Concord, and at the libraries of Henniker and Londonderry.

The couple had five children, four boys and one girl. Legend has it that James Wallace died young and left Mary a widow in care of all five children. In the meantime, Don Pedro had given up his pirate life and rowed up the Contoocook River to a parcel of land where his ship carpenters built a beautiful home for him. Much of the home itself resembled his trusty pirate ship. As it turns out, Don Pedro was actually an English nobleman-turned-privateer through Letter of Marque—who was given six thousand acres of land by the King of England, but preferred the exciting and dangerous life as a swashbuckler on the high seas. Now still young and prosperous, he settled on his vast tract of territory that later became present day Henniker, New Hampshire.

News of Mary's plight reached the ears of the former buccaneer and he beseeched that she come live with him and he would care for her and her children. Some say she married the man and there are others who swear that Don Pedro had given up piracy earlier and changed his name to James Wallace, then married Mary. No matter what the turn of events were, Mary lived in the home of Don Pedro and cared for him.

One night, a few old friends of Don Pedro paid a visit on them. There was much conversation and Mary paid no heed to the unruly guests. All of a sudden she heard a shout and then the voice of Don Pedro cursing the other men. Mary went out back where she saw Don Pedro lying in the yard with a cutlass still in him. She removed the sword and before he died he told her where he had hidden all the gold and jewels he had amassed from his earlier profession. He also requested that she bury him under the hearth of the fireplace so he could always be there to look out for her. She did as he wanted and lived the rest of her life in the house. She was ninety-four years old when she died on February 15, 1814. She is presently buried in the Williams lot in Henniker's Centre Cemetery behind the town hall now called The Community Building. The stone is adorned with the traditional weeping willow and urn that were popular for that period.

The inscription reads,

"IN MEMORY OF WIDOW MARY WALLACE WHO DIED FEB. 15 A.D. 1814 IN THE 94TH YEAR OF HER AGE."

Her grave is easy to spot twelve rows back with a special plaque in front of it that reads, "OCEAN BORN MARY."

The story does not end there. Her spirit remained in the house after her death. Many people claimed to have seen a tall red-headed woman in the windows of the old house when it was unoccupied. People claim that they have seen her ghost in a spectral horse drawn carriage moving towards the house. State Police once reported seeing Mary's wraith crossing the road in front of her house.

In 1917, Louis Roy and his mother purchased the house and opened it to the public for tours at a fee. His claims of Mary's ghost being present in the house captured the attention of everybody from magazines to thrill seekers looking for pirates and treasure. Not only did a rocking chair move back and forth on its own volition when guests walked by it, but Louis, or "Gus" as he was also known, also rented shovels for fifty cents each so people could have a chance at finding the gold Don Pedro had buried in the yard.

Both he and his mother had claimed to see Mary's spirit on many occasions descending the staircase and disappearing into thin air. During the hurricane of 1938, Mr. Roy noticed the garage he had built was swaying dangerously in the wind. He went out and found some long timber to support the sides. When he returned to the safety of his home his mother asked who was helping him. He was quite shocked as he did the job quite alone at the time. She swore she saw a tall red-haired girl in a white gown helping him with the boards. She then started to follow him into the house but vanished just before crossing the threshold.

Later Mr. Roy would meet up with the ghost of Mary Wallace again when a fierce storm overtook the region.

He claimed that she saved his life nineteen times during his struggle to hold his buildings together during the great Nor'easter. The Roy family held tours of the house well into the 1960s before it changed hands. David and Corinne Russell then took ownership of the house. Mrs. Russell had cared for Mr. Roy in his old age and knew well of the history of the house as Mr. Roy told her everything he knew about the now famous landmark. Those words are tales to be told in another time. Let us keep with the ghostly encounters for now.

During the Russell's tenure in the house, a caretaker accidentally dropped a kerosene heater down the stairs and caught the wall and staircase on fire. Having no running water in the house, Mr. Russell dashed out into the snow to grab some in order to quench the flames. When he returned, the massive fire was out. His wife, watching in disbelief, related how the flames just quickly died down and smothered in a mysterious manner. They were sure that the ghost of Mary Wallace had a role in the uncanny occurrence.

One visitor came to the house and was greeted by a tall woman in eighteenth century attire. The woman who answered the door said that the house was a mess and the owners were not home at the time. The guest thought she looked rather strange in appearance but heeded her words and left. Later, when she returned, she was informed that no such person exists in the house, at least not in the physical realm. Her ghost is still reported to this day, wandering the grounds of the house. She is often seen by the well in the yard.

There are claims that the Ocean Born Mary House is not really where she lived. It is also stated that those claims are just calls for privacy by the present owners of the estate. Either way, the accounts have survived centuries of change and elaboration, as have the spirits, regardless of their actual domicile. Because they are private homes, Arlene and I did not bother to invade their solitude. There are enough stories about to satisfy the most ravenous appetite for adventure.

That is the legend of the pirate Don Pedro and Ocean Born Mary. It is perhaps the greatest legend that has ever emanated from the mouths of New Englanders. As for the whereabouts of Don Pedro, he is reported buried still, under the hearthstone where he last requested to lie. People visiting the house have had strange feelings when near the hearthstone of the fireplace. Some claim to have felt vibrations when touching it. As I researched further, I talked to some old timers who had lived in Henniker. They told me that a few witnesses claimed to have seen a man in strange garb much like that of a nobleman, standing near the fireplace. Could it be the wraith of the great privateer still watching over his domain? Many have even seen the ghost of Don Pedro near the house and yard where his cache has supposedly remained hidden deep within the earth. Perhaps he is watching over the treasure in hopes that Mary might still be in need. Even in death.

The Ghostly Crew
of the Charles Haskell

When I was about eleven years old, I took a book out of the Greenville Public Library on ghosts. One of the stories became etched in my memory forever recalling itself to the forefront each time I would visit the shores of New England's coastline. The eerie accounts of the *Charles Haskell* and its fated crew stand to this day as one of the reasons why New England harbors some of the scariest ghost stories one could ever hold a candle to.

The *Charles Haskell* was built in 1869. She was a beautiful schooner that any captain would be proud to sail. Tragedy beset the boat before it was launched. A workman making one last inspection slipped and broke his neck. Such ill omen can really taint a vessel. The original purchaser immediately backed out of the sale and the schooner sat dormant until a brave captain purchased the boat and set sail for Georges Bank with his crew.

That winter, as the ship was anchored in the fishing grounds of Georges Bank, a terrible storm blew in. There sat many other fishing vessels moored in the bountiful shoals. The captain feared other boats might loose their anchor lines and smash into the *Haskell.* He ordered the lines cut for maneuvering purposes. This proved to be a fatal move as the ship crashed into another schooner, the *Andrew Johnson* out of Salem. The Salem vessel sank quickly, taking all ten crewmembers to their graves. The *Charles Haskell* was damaged but stayed afloat.

A few months later, the fishing boat was back in Georges Bank again. The crew fished for several days undisturbed until one night when the most terrifying incident changed their lives forever. As the midnight air descended to an intolerable chill, ten phantom fishermen in oilskins floated over the railing of the boat and silently began manning the nets, baiting unseen hooks, and going about the tasks of a well-seasoned angler. Captain Clifford Curtis and his crew stared in disbelief at the apparitions. At one point, the captain mustered enough courage to approach the specters but was immediately froze in his tracks when they turned towards him with black holes of the dead for eyes and unearthly disdain on their face.

The ghostly crew resumed their duties until dawn. At that point they climbed over the railings and vanished into the sea. The *Charles Haskell* sailed at breakneck speed for the Port of Gloucester. Unfortunately, breakneck speed in those days was not enough for them to reach dry land safely before another night saw them in the company of the phantom fishermen once more. This time, as the crew pulled in their lines, they climbed over the railings while staring at the captain and began walking across the water towards Salem Harbor.

Once in port, the schooner was hastily abandoned and never saw the fishing grounds of Georges Bank again. Some say that the *Charles Haskell* sat in Gloucester port until it fell into ruin, as no one would dare board the haunted ship. Another account states that a Novia Scotia merchant purchased the vessel and took it away. Either way Gloucester was rid of its haunted schooner. As for what became of the ten ghostly crewmembers, many who fish Georges Bank will tell you that sometimes they see things or receive help from unseen hands. Perhaps the spirits are looking for passage back to Salem where they too can finally come to port after such a long time at sea.

Jewell Island

Jewell Island is among the many islands that litter the Casco Bay area of Maine. They were once called the "Calendar Islands" because it was said to be three hundred and sixty-five landmasses jutting from the water. Two hundred to two hundred and twenty have been reportedly inventoried depending on your view of what constitutes an island. Jewell Island has a history of blood and booty. Because of this, it is haunted.

It was reported settled by a gruff Barnstable fishing master named George Jewell. It is written that he traded some gunpowder, rum, and fishing implements to the Indians for the atoll and lived there as a recluse. He met his demise in Boston Harbor where he drowned after too much froth and fun. The island still runs rampant with the spirits of pirates and other such scurvy kin. Being eight miles out from the shoreline of Portland, it makes sense that seafaring sort would seek it out in turn. There are designated campsites and trails on the state-owned property. There are also two towers from World War II standing about sixty-to-eighty feet tall. Visitors are frequent to the island as they have been for centuries. Some of those centuries-old visitors are permanent fixtures on Jewell Island.

Captain Kidd is said to have buried treasure here and still haunts the area. A man procured a map supposedly drawn by Captain Kidd. His name was George Vigny and he came from St. John, New Brunswick, in search of the buried treasure around 1860. At the time, a less than scrupulous man named Elijah Jones lived on Jewell Island. They somehow hooked up and became digging partners. Soon, Jones was rich and the other man was never seen again. When questioned about the St. John man, Jones told people that they were unsuccessful in finding any treasure and he went home.

Curious folk wandered out to the island where they found a large hole on the south cove with the square imprint of a great chest at the bottom. From then on, people began to see a hideous, human form with glaring green eyes and blood dripping from his mouth whenever they came towards the area. The islanders even poured lamb's blood around the spot in order to exorcise the demon that they believed Jones and Vigny may have unearthed during their plunders.

The horror did not confine itself to just the cove where the chest was taken. Jones's home was prone to screams and moans permeating the midnight air. Windows and glassware would smash to pieces in front of stunned guests. His house was forever a haven for hell. The wealthy but haunted Jones lived into his older age and died in the late 1800s. It was thought that he was a pirate and rum smuggler. As for being a killer, a farmer happened upon a skeleton wedged in a crevice while plowing his land. Older locals recognized the distinctive ring on the bony hand with the initials G. V. as that of the man from St. John. The horrible wraith was no longer seen after that, but the area still reverberates with an interminable haunt. As one walks by the site where the treasure was found, peculiar lights and creepy groans emanate from the cove. One can hear the sound of shovels, chopping into the sand, echoing through the sea air, sending a chill down the bravest of men's spines. Who are the glowing diggers of plunder? Is it the original buccaneers that hid the loot, or is it the ghosts of Jones and his unfortunate comrade, destined to live out that evil moment of money and murder throughout all eternity?

The ghosts of seven other pirates are said to roam the island as well. Female pirate Anne Bonney was reported to have buried a stash on the island. After her men finished the task, she killed them with her pistols and cutlass. Many frightened visitors to the isle have seen their ghosts wandering amidst the wooded area and shoreline. Seven graves with small markers were discovered in the 1960s. Perhaps they are the final resting spots of the bandits. Unfortunately, they do not seem to be at rest.

Pirates and rogues are not the only ghouls haunting the landscape of Jewell Island. In 1977, Margaret Newlin, then fifteen years old, visited the island with her family. She was no stranger to the bay outcroppings as her father worked as a compass adjuster among the islets. During World War II, Jewell was one of the islands used as a garrison for the Navy. There are gun batteries and tunnels where the remains of a fort once held vigil over the Casco Bay. She often played among the remains as her father performed his duties. As she wandered along the island's many trails that summer day in 1977, a chilling spectacle awaited her. She came to a tunnel that led to a gun platform. She suddenly heard voices coming from the small duct leading to the gunnery. At first she assumed it was other adventurers exploring the historical ruins. She called in but received no reply. As she stood several yards from the entrance, she was suddenly thrown into alarm as three countenances in old uniforms and helmets emerged from the hollow. One wore wire-rimmed glasses reminiscent of the 1930s or 1940s. They approached her as if she did not exist.

She stood there frozen in fear as the phantom soldiers meandered by her then faded before her eyes.

She rushed back to her family ranting about her paranormal beholding but they did not believe her; at first. Belief came years later as they began to hear other accounts of the ghostly crew still manning the batteries of Jewell Island. No one knows the exact identity of the ghostly gunners. There were about five hundred soldiers stationed on the island during the war. Perhaps there are more than just the three Margaret saw. Who knows what strange things lie deep in the tunnels that circulate below the surface of the haunted sands of Jewell Island? Phantom soldiers, buried treasure, ghostly pirates, and apparitions of adventurers met with evil ends might be just some of the unearthly residents awaiting the arrival of the unsuspecting traveler. If you decide to hike or camp on Jewell Island, keep your eyes wide and your ears unfolded, for what lurks about might make a believer out of you if not a permanent resident as well.

The Sea Bird

Many eerie accounts in history become lost in the shuffle of legend and folklore. All too often they fall second fiddle to another spectacular event. In time, their incident is but a faded recollection of another era, occasionally recanted by the oldest of the village, while reclining next to a crackling wood stove in the back corner of the local general store. I shall now recall to the anxious reader, the nearly forgotten but true accounts of the *Sea Bird*.

The exact date of the mysterious occurrence is of speculation. One account puts it at 1733. Another more popular account gives us the year 1750. Both are consistent with the month of October. It would be reasonable to assume that the date of the peculiar incident you are about to peruse was 1750. Ship owner and Newport merchant, Isaac Stelle is on record as purchasing a beautiful hand-made desk and bookcase from furniture maker Christopher Townsend in 1742 for sixty-five pounds. Given this sale and events that follow, it seems more feasible that the *Sea Bird* met with the supernatural in October of 1750.

Either way, Stelle, among others huddled at Newport's Easton Point, eagerly awaiting the arrival of his ship the *Sea Bird*. In those days, the successful homecoming of a merchant ship was a paramount affair. Family members and friends rejoiced the safe return their loved ones.

Captain Johnathon Huxham was her commander. The *Sea Bird* was returning from a successful business venture in Bristol, England. (Some writings say they were returning from the south.) Fishermen, who had spotted the craft the evening before, reported the crew and vessel in good health. They felt no worry of its impending arrival in the morning. As the ship came into view, the crowd grew elated. The lofty schooner, with her sails full of wind and moving at a sound clip, continued to bear down towards land. People began to notice that the boat was yawing a bit. It just avoided "The Ledge" at the mouth of the Narragansett Harbor. It also reeled by other navigation hazards as it headed towards Newport Harbor at full sail. Perhaps it was the captain performing aquatic stunts out of glee and relief of his return. At some point, the sails should have been taken up but no such endeavor transpired. The ship was now heading straight for the wharf as the frightened throng wondered what the crew was trying to do.

The *Sea Bird* took a small sudden turn as if heading up the bay away from Newport. At that point, she came so close to shore that people began to cringe in expectation of a collision. As the craft passed by them, they all beheld an eerie sight. No one was at the helm, yet the boat had thrice maneuvered out of the path of eminent destruction. Her deck was void of any human form as she ran towards the beach on the north side of the wharf. Moments seemed like eons as the *Sea Bird* finally came to a crashing halt on the beach near the point where the astonished mass stood.

Immediately, boats were dispatched and men boarded the grounded ship. To their amazement, the only living creatures aboard the *Sea Bird* were a dog and a cat. The dog, wagging his tail, was happy to see the perplexed band of rescuers. Amidst the creaking of the beached brig, a whistling sound emanated. It turned out to be a boiling kettle in the galley on a freshly stoked stove. The table was set for breakfast and food had been laid out but not eaten.

The condition of the captain's quarters ripened the mystery. Captain Huxham's dressing gown lay at the foot of the cabin stairs. A fair sum of gold coins were strewn upon his desk and there was written papers stating that the ship had entered Rhode Island waters, and was heading past Point Judith on route to Newport Harbor but a few miles away. The only item missing from his cabin was the logbook. The searchers also noticed one of the long boats missing from the side of the ship.

What became of the crew and longboat? No bodies or wreckage ever washed ashore anywhere in the area. None of the men, including Newport native Captain Huxham, First Mate Rundall, another young Newport man on his first sea voyage, the cook, and four other crew members were ever heard from again. There was no sign of a struggle. The ship was clean of any blood or signs of foul play. Yet, the crew had literally vanished under the noses of their fellow citizens.

The *Sea Bird* was repaired and sold to Henry Collins. He renamed it the *Beach Bird*. She made many more voyages but reports aboard the ship of ghostly figures moving about made it difficult to secure a steady crew. The wage aboard a merchant vessel was enough to make many a man brave the unknown both at sea and aboard. In time, the haunted vessel sat in Newport Harbor, all but sunken at the mooring where she had last come to port. The Revolutionary War saw the occupation of Newport by the British. They raised the sulking hulk and converted the ghost ship into an armed galley where she saw new life once more. From there, her fate fades into time and legend.

The narrative of the *Sea Bird* conjures up the hair on many a horrified heeder's neck. It is said that a duo among the crew murdered the rest and threw them overboard just shy of Point Judith, then abandoned the ship only hours before the ghost vessel ran aground. No one was ever seen rowing ashore and no remnants—either intact or in pieces—were ever reported of the *Sea Bird's* long boat. As one stares out off of Easton Point, it can only be wondered to this day what ghastly fate gripped the crew of the *Sea Bird*. Are those seagulls echoing in the wind or the screams of the past trying to divulge a truth only the sea knows for sure?

The *Sea Bird* came by Brenton Point and at some point in this vicinity, the crew vanished without a trace.

The Bird Island Light

As the sun sets on Sippican Harbor in Buzzard's Bay off of Marion, Massachusetts, a bright light flashes in six second intervals. The curious might take a spyglass and get a better glimpse of the source that illuminates the waters for that brief moment. It is the Bird Island Light. If one looks close enough, they just might spy another illumination on the rocky two-acre isle. It is the ghost of Sarah Moore, wife of the first light keeper of the Bird Island Light.

The light station was established in 1819. The first keepers were William Moore and his wife Sarah. William Moore served in the War of 1812. Some claim he was a privateer-turned-pirate. Others, according to record, say he was a paymaster for the war. One thing is certain. He owed the U. S. Army money. Whether it was from freebooting or free taking, he had to pay for his deeds. He was reportedly put at the lighthouse with no boat to secure a possible escape. Provisions were brought to the isolated atoll on a scheduled basis. The island seemed cursed from the start. The first winter brought a severe gale. The intensity of the storm swept everything that was not secured dearly off the island. The frightened light keeper and his family had to retreat to the tower as the waters rose over the island enveloping the keeper's home. The island remained under water for much of the day.

It is known that Moore performed experiments on the island concerning the use of whale oil for heating purposes and the perfection of "air boxes." These could be built into ships to keep them from sinking. Or, perhaps a person could use one to float away in the dark stealth of the night without being seen.

Mrs. Moore was a heavy tobacco smoker. Her incessant addiction was known well on the mainland. William was not happy over her smoking and told many it would be the death of her. One day, in 1832, the distress flag called authorities to the island. Upon arriving, they found Sarah Moore dead. Mr. Moore told them she died of tuberculosis and was contagious. The authorities, not wanting to suffer from the highly contagious disease, left it at that. He buried his wife on the island in an undisclosed place. Soon the talk of ill will began to rattle about on the mainland. Many stated that William Moore often hit his wife and possibly killed her. Police went back to the island to question Moore, but he had disappeared, never to be seen again.

It was not long after this bizarre occurrence that later keepers began to see the manifestation of a hunched over old woman. The second keeper began to see the wraith of the woman at his door. One night a slight rapping on the door roused the keeper. When he opened it, to his horror, he came face to face with an old woman holding her hand out in a beckoning manner. She then reeled backwards towards the sea with a pitiful look on her face. Soon the unearthly knock became a portent of terror, as the keeper's family knew well it was the old woman's ghost looking for her alleged murderer.

In 1889-1890, the original keeper's house was torn down and a gun with a bag containing tobacco and a note was discovered. Some thought it to be the murder weapon. Others believed Moore used it to keep his sick wife from summoning help. The note accompanying the gun blamed certain local denizens for supplying the tobacco that put a dreadful end to his "dearly loved" wife.

The strange discovery and new house did not put the spirit of Mrs. Moore in repose. Keeper after keeper would cringe at the faint rapping on the door, knowing what unearthly guise stood beyond its threshold. Some would hear the knocking and answer the beckoning rap only to find the entrance void of any form. The smell of tobacco would pervade their nostrils along with the ocean air. Others would see the countenance float by a room, followed by the same musty tobacco odor. Needless to say, many keepers were relieved to be released from their tour of duty at the haunted beacon.

In 1890, the eleven-month-old child of keeper Peter Murray grew ill with pneumonia. The heavy ice and treacherous weather kept the panic stricken keeper from securing help. In a final act of desperation, he extinguished the light. By the time help was able to brave the elements and get to the lighthouse, it was too late. The baby had died. The family buried the child on the mainland and never again set foot on the haunted Bird Island.

The light was finally decommissioned on June 15, 1933. The Cape Cod Canal with its lighted buoys had made the decrepit signal obsolete. The only movement on the island from that point on was the nesting birds of the sea, and the visage of an old woman wandering among the deserted buildings. The hurricane of 1938 destroyed every building on the island save for the light tower. Even the large fog bell tower was seen being washed into the sea by the worst hurricane in modern times.

Now the renovated light tower sits as a lonely icon of the island's history. Its only other historical entity is Sarah Moore who is still occasionally seen beckoning to the passerby with a pleading outstretched hand. The poignant appearance on her face is either due her untimely demise, or the sad state of the last life she knew.

The Sea Goin' Coffin

I have heard this narrative several times and have enjoyed its recanting in many of the towns along the New England shoreline. It seems that the amusing enchantment of the story overshadows the black theme of death. Presented now is a legend from Maine that everyone should hold within the crevices of their memory.

Along the Maine coast there be an ancient tale told of a man named Captain Zachariah. He was not only the local boat builder, but had his hand at constructing coffins when the townsfolk saw the unfortunate need. The captain's aunt was old and near death. The family pleaded the old captain, up in years himself, to make haste and construct a coffin for proper burial.

Time passed and no coffin had been produced. The absent-minded captain was deep in his favorite pastime, the creation of sailing vessels. He had totally forgotten about the coffin. The family became insistent on a burial box, as the matriarch was fading fast. Ole' Zach apologized for his absent-mindedness, as he was so wrapped up in the work on a new rudder for a thirty-foot schooner. He was obliged to have the casket completed and delivered within a few "morrows."

A few days passed and a wagon came to a halt in front of the family's house with a freshly made coffin. The looks of relief turned to bewilderment as the family ogled the strange sarcophagus complete, with centerboard and a ship's rudder attached to it. Old Captain Zachariah was either short of mind, hurrying time, or out to teach them a lesson.

The Charles W. Morgan

Although the *Charles W. Morgan's* whaling days ended in 1921 after eighty years of service, some of her crew still seem to be on the job. This comes from several witnesses who have seen a phantom form skulking about the forward room where huge cauldrons turned whale blubber into oil for lamps.

The *Charles W. Morgan* was built in 1841 by Jethro and Zachariah Hillman of New Bedford, Massachusetts. It is presently a treasured exhibit at the Mystic Seaport Museum of America and the Sea, in Mystic, Connecticut. She is the last of her kind. The all-wood whaling ship is one hundred and thirteen feet long by seventeen and one half feet deep. Her main mast stretches one hundred and ten feet above the deck with up to thirteen thousand square feet of sail. The history of the ship and the men who made their living from the whaling vessel is as fascinating as the fact that it is reported haunted.

Crews spent up to five years at sea in hopes of attaining the precious oil that sent a glow through night air in the nineteenth and early twentieth centuries. Although gas streetlights were installed in London in 1814, and kerosene lamps were in use in Germany after 1853, whale oil lamps were commonplace in American homes. They remained for quite some time. Kerosene lamps eventually made their way to the states, and Thomas Edison invented the practical light bulb in 1879. One year later, Broadway in New York City was lit up with Edison's bright idea. Yet many people who owned oil lamps still relied on the whaling trade for illumination of their homes.

The dangers aboard a whaling ship were certainly genuine. Many whalers lost their lives in the adventurous undertaking. Perhaps it is one of these past anglers of the great mammal, still lingering on board the floating museum. He has been spied smoking a pipe while reclining among the ropes of the ship. Phantom voices of the past have been heard in the forecastle where the crew slept. Each time the perceiver of the utterances went to investigate, the cramped unpalatable living quarters were void of the living. The museum itself is not promoting the ship as haunted. That would be putting too much to conjecture on the side of the ghostly reports.

Curators told me that the stories related to them coincide with uncanny resemblance, but nothing out of the ordinary has happened to any of the staff. They seem more interested in relaying the history of the *Charles W. Morgan* as opposed to the lingering spirits that might still be on duty. The ship's history is undeniably worth reading about. They invite you to visit the wondrous vessel and draw your own conclusion. Creaks and noises are quite common on an old wooden boat. So are ghosts, as I have learned.

The *Charles W. Morgan*.

Arlene and I spent a cool January day at the historic seaport. Even if there were no ghosts to be seen that day, the spirit of the site transports one back in time to an era where artisans skillfully crafted every item imaginable by hand. Blacksmith shops and taverns lace the lanes along with old time variety and drug stores. The many buildings are laid out along small streets overlooking the ships that are docked for all to board and roam the decks. Of all the places we have been, this is truly one of the most memorable.

We boarded the *Charles W. Morgan* and immediately felt a rush of something quite different overtake us. It was an experience of a lifetime alone just being on the last of its kind. We went downstairs where captains bunk, galley, blubber room, and forecastle or foc's'tle was. I began recording for EVPs while Arlene took pictures of the areas in question. The day was foggy and heavy drizzle kept the usual flow of tourists from venturing out to the historic site. We were alone on the ship, save for a staff member housed in a small, heated room on deck. We roamed the decks and levels of the Morgan for about an hour. The reported spirits of the *Morgan* probably felt the same as the many who did not venture out that day. They were nowhere to be heard or seen.

Despite the lack of paranormal phenomena, we still had an experience worth the trip. The sights and attractions are an incredible learning experience, and the other ships were no less intriguing. The *Morgan,* buildings, and other ships in the vast museum site are open for tours and are a must for those who have a penchant for history and mystery. On July 21, 1977, the *Charles W. Morgan* became a National Historic Landmark and is considered the museum's most treasured item. The spectral crew still on board has thought that for almost two hundred years.

The ropes await another reclining whaler from a long gone era.

Looking out to port from the *Charles W. Morgan* as one would have in the nineteenth century.

The Minerva's Prophetic Foretelling

Premonitions can come in various forms. Some are feelings, others in the form of dreams. Some omens arrive in the appearance of a ghastly countenance. These forbearers of tragedy are the most fearful of all. This next account falls into the realm of phantom ships although not so much the ship as the phantom itself. I am more than confident the reader will find this next chronicle a thriller. As you read through the next few pages, try not to shudder as the hair on the back of your neck begins to reach for the heavens.

Jeffery Richardson went to his bedchamber on March 3, 1787. It was as uneventful as any other evening after the sun had quit its vigil on the land. He slept quite soundly until three in the morning when he was abruptly churned from his slumber by a presence in his room. The voice called to him. He recognized the resonance of its bay almost immediately. It was his brother-in-law Captain James Scott. His sister Mary's husband was the commander of the brig, *Minerva*. This would have not been such a terrible incident as his sister had been staying with Mr. Richardson and his wife. Therefore it was reasonable for the voice of Scott to be heard or his presence seen around the house. What gave Jeffery Richardson his gasping demeanor was the fact that Captain Scott had steered the *Minerva* out of port earlier that evening. How was it possible for the commander to be standing in his room? The semi-transparent form never gave him an answer as it faded into the darkness.

Richardson quickly woke his wife, but the apparition had already vanished. He told his wife of the bizarre occurrence but she just scolded him, owing it to a bad dream. Jeffery Richardson knew better. His terror was confirmed when the voice of his brother-in-law broke the silence of the night air once more. The chilling pleas of the captain made him shudder. He quickly donned some proper attire then unlatched the door to get a glimpse into the darkness. The region was in the midst of a blinding blizzard. The snow fell hard and fast, marooning everything in its path. Richardson returned to his wife who was now awake and concerned about her husband's sincere convictions.

Although he lay back to slumber, sleep eluded him until the shafts of morning's light trickled through the cracks of the window shutters. Richardson then arose and prepared himself for the trek to the shores of Marshfield where the *Minerva* had set sail the previous evening. Within an hour he was upon the beach where he beheld the most dreadful sight. Great mounds of wreckage lay asunder along the windswept dunes. Bodies were washing ashore as the local folk tried to gather them in the terrible, but waning storm.

As the depth of the tragedy unfolded in front of him, Richardson was told there were no survivors found. The name of the ship remained a mystery as no quarterboard had yet washed ashore. It was then suggested that he search in the vicinity of the Cut River for clues of the identity of the doomed brig. As he reached his destination, other men were salvaging what they could from the mystery wreck. He found a piece of quarterboard. The letters "VA" were visible. As he rummaged around some more, he found another piece with the letters, "INER" on it. His head sank in grief as he recalled the early morning hours when the wraith of his brother-in-law cried to him in such a desperate unearthly tone.

It would be sometime later in the day before Captain Scott's body was recovered from the surf. He was pulled from the unforgiving sea and brought to a nearby church. The only way they could identify the badly surf-beaten captain was by his distinctive pocket watch. The *Minerva* had gone down while still in sight of the Richardson house. The ghostly visitation of Captain Scott was about the time the ship broke to pieces and sank. No one forgot that fateful day in Marshfield. Least of all, Jeffery Richardson, who laid witness to the phantom captain and his final pleas. To this day the residents of Marshfield can hear the screams and the breaking up of the ghostly ship when the March winds howl across the water to the shore, and the spirits of the *Minerva* relive that final moment that is etched in all time.

The account of Captain Scott's ghostly visitation to his brother-in-law lives on in a testament to this tragedy. Jeffery Richardson never swore to any less. In his latest of years, he still recalled with exact recollection the night the phantom voice called out to him.

The Palatine Light

There are many truths and legends concerning the Palatine Light. It becomes difficult for the investigator to sort through the validity of what really happened, and the poetic license shrouding the enigma that has relived in the waters off of Block Island for centuries. Some of the hardcore proof of the incident lies in the land along the Southwestern edge of the island where a marker was erected as a memorial during the last century. It simply reads, "Palatine Graves-1738." The other proof lies out to sea when the fiery ghost ship makes its appearance after Christmas on or around December 27th of each year. From these evidences, we can begin to look back on what is known as the most talked about ghost ship on the American seas, the *Palatine Light*.

John Greenleaf Whittier immortalized the event in his 1867 poem, "The Palatine Light." This gives rise to why the ship is often mistaken for that name. Its actual known name was the *Princess Augusta*. When the verse first surfaced, islanders were up in arms of the tainted picture it painted as to the fate of the ship that has haunted the waters for centuries. They were certainly not happy with Whittier's use of poetic license.

Some accounts state that the ship made its fatal run in 1732. The graves and other sources show that it was 1738. The brigantine was sailing back and forth before 1738. The *Princess Augusta* did make a run to America in 1736. It deposited German Palatinates in the colonies bound for Pennsylvania. The record of their journey and who made it still exists in the Philadelphia's historic archives. The record, compiled by Ted Von Mechow puts the date at September 13, 1736.

It would appear that the *Princess Augusta* made only a few trips across the Atlantic with the same purpose. It did not sail in 1737 due to damage she sustained on her maiden voyage. Mr. Von Mechow related to me that the ship was damaged as it entered the Delaware Bay. A passenger was found dead in the water a few days later. It is presumed he may have fallen overboard when the boat hit whatever caused the damage. The repairs delayed the vessel's return to Europe. It is reported that she left Rotterdam once more in 1738 with about 340 Palatinates looking for a new life. The three-mast brigantine under the command of Captain George Long, hoisted from its mooring on an eternal adventure that has, to this day, no conclusion.

Once the ship was at sea, it is said that the water supply went bad and food became scarce. According to legend, one of the first to reportedly die was the captain. First Mate Andrew Brook took charge. Some records state that Brook was the captain from the start. Either way he was the captain at some point. His navigation skills were very lacking as the ship took a wrong course in heading for their destination. The situation about the vessel began to deteriorate. Half the crew was dead from the poisoned water and many of the passengers as well. It was told that the crew began to steal money from the passengers and ration small amounts of food for excessive wages. Those who could not pay for their meager means died of starvation. Their troubles were just beginning.

While wandering the sea, a fierce blizzard bore down upon the hapless hoard. Starvation, dehydration, and frostbite were their main enemies at this point. After the storm had abated, the decks were frozen in mounds of snow and ice. The ship was hard to keep on course due to the frozen sails. Stories of what happened next begin to vary. Some say that a crewmember saw a light in the distance and they steered towards it. As they raced full speed, they realized it was not a signal fire but the work of wreckers who made their living luring ships to an impending doom. The ship could not steer clear of the rocky ledges and smashed into the cliffs below the false signal fire. Once the ship was broken up on the rocks, the wreckers came down and stole everything of value from it and left the passengers for dead. This is one account of what happened to the *Princess Augusta*.

An account written on the history of Block Island in *Tales of New England Past*, edited by Frank Oppel, states that the ship ran aground after the crew supposedly abandoned it, probably knowing they had committed an outright act of piracy against the passengers. The islanders saw the disaster and rushed to the ship to help. They rescued all aboard. The vessel had suffered very little damage and was still seaworthy. The islanders then towed the brigantine out to safer waters but one woman would not leave the boat. It is not known exactly why. It is claimed that she had gone insane. Perhaps she wanted the ship as restitution for her pirated possessions.

Once safely in high water, the islanders tended to the rest of the passengers. Some died from the horrible results of their predicament and were buried on the island. In the meantime, during the hours after the tolling of the midnight bell, a blaze was seen off shore. The *Princess Augusta* was on fire. Many think the woman knocked over a lantern setting the boat aflame. No one will ever know for sure. As the brigantine met its fiery end, terrible shrieks from the boat could be heard permeating the midnight air. In almost no time, the deep claimed the ship and its lone passenger.

Two years later, the *Princess Augusta* appeared on the horizon. At first no one really paid much heed to the fast approaching ship, but when it failed to furl its sails, panic broke out. The people watched in terror as the vessel raced full speed for the cliffs. Just before it reached the shore, it burst into flames and vanished. One year later, the tall ship was spied racing towards the shore only to burst into flames and vanish once more.

The citizens of Block Island knew it was the *Princess Augusta* come back to relive that fateful moment when no one could save her from her fiery demise. Almost every year since, the phantom ship has been spotted ablaze off the coast of Block Island. It has been seen by countless generations. Its ethereal blaze shimmers with the same unearthly intensity today as it did in 1738. It is common knowledge to the seafarers in the area that when the ghostly glow of the ship rises out of the deep, they must retreat in haste for the safety of land, or their ship and its crew will surely be dragged to a watery grave.

The Isadore

Thomas King had dreams of grave demeanor. The dreams were more a harbinger of death than a nightmare. Every bone in his body trembled at the horrible omen that was to come, yet he had already received advanced wages for his journey aboard the merchant ship, the *Isadore*. The four-hundred-ton bark was to set sail from Kennebunkport that evening en route to New Orleans. Captain Leander Foss had paid every crewmember in advance so their families could endure in their absence. Tom approached the captain with his forewarning. He had premonitions of seven black coffins laid side by side on the wharf at Kennebunkport. In one of the dreams, he spied the monikers on the burial boxes. Each bore a name of the *Isadore* crew. An ethereal voice broke through the eerie hum saying, "One of these is for you." The captain was unsympathetic to his fears and fiercely ordered him on ship at departure time. As he left the office, it became clear that the death bark was worse than the captain's bite.

It was Thanksgiving day, 1842, and the crew celebrated in port with flagons of ale and rum as the ship rolled down the railway to the water. Something then suddenly made the whole crowd numb with silence. As the *Isadore* slipped into the brine, it listed and attempted to capsize. Many men rushed to the boat and steadied the bark until it sat well in the water. It was now ready to be boarded. The crew was a bit apprehensive over this ill omen. Jack Haley turned to Thomas King and told him of a dream he had of imminent disaster and death to the ship and its crew. This was all Tom needed to hear. His fears were certainly substantiated by the other crewmember's nightmares.

When it came time to set sail, Captain Foss assembled his crew and found only twelve of the thirteen sailors had traversed the gangplank. Thomas King was on the roster but not on board. Feeling cheated out of his wages, the angry Foss initiated a search for the deserter and crook. They searched for King everywhere but could not find him. The captain finally called the rest of his men on board and sailed without King. He reckoned he would deal with him later. That would never be. As they left port, a terrible storm began to rage with blinding snow and howling winds. The next morning, wreckage of the bark began to wash ashore. Seven bodies were found as well. One was Jack Haley. There were no survivors. The other crewmembers were never found. Some believe they sank to the deep depths under a rocky abyss called "The Pulpit."

The whole village went into mourning. A few days later, they were elated to see a lone figure emerge among them. It was Thomas King. He had appeared at the door of his home tired and hungry. His astonished wife asked how he survived. He then told her of his dreams and how he hid in the woods until the ship was out to sea. He felt ashamed and cowardly for his actions. When he found out the bark had wrecked, he was quite taken aback. Some townspeople thought he was justified in his proceedings, as his dreams were forewarnings by God. Others thought him a coward and shied from his company from then on.

Several years later, a strange ship was spotted sailing past Avery Cove near Boon Island off the coast of Kennebunkport. Fishermen recognized the bark as the ghostly countenance of the *Isadore*. Many have seen the phantom vessel sailing through the water with no sound. Some have sailed close enough to throw a line to the bark. Each time another sailing vessel got close, the *Isadore* would disappear. Those who spy the misty ship will swear that it vanishes just as it hits Avery Cove. That is where the original *Isadore* met its gruesome fate in 1842. Light keepers of Cape Neddick (Nubble Light) and Boon Island Light have witnessed the ghostly floater since. To this day, the shadowy craft still roams the waters off of Kennebunkport. Those who witness the ghost boat can attest to this. Those who have not, wait in fearful expectation of that moment when the ominous silhouette appears on the horizon possibly come back to reclaim its missing crewmember.

Looking for the ghost ship *Isadore* from the cliffs of Cape Neddick near Nubble Light. Note Boon Island and lighthouse barely visible in the far distance.

Blackbeard's Ghost

What legend be known that has not sprouted from the seeds of truth, reveling in its larger than life fruits, ripened for the harvest of eternal tale? The stories of pirates and their adventures have many a frothing fable swirling in the whirlpool of facts. It is hard to disaffiliate much of the written truths and folklore of these bandits of the briny. The best we can do is take all the data and draw our own conclusion as to what we think is real and what might be embellished yarns spun over tankards in seaside pubs. Such are the accounts of Blackbeard. His life and death are swathed in illustrious narrations. How many are accurate? That I cannot say, but as these stories unfold, it will become evident that he is as large a legend in death as he was in life.

Blackbeard's real name has become a matter of inference over the years. For the past few centuries, written accounts state the fierce pirate as Edward Teach. Early writings shortly after his demise say his real name was Thatch. It is not clear where he was born or when. Some writings claim Bristol, England, some say London. There is even an account where he was said to hail from Philadelphia, Pennsylvania. Captain Charles Johnson wrote much about Blackbeard in a 1724 second edition of his famous pirate biography. This text seems to hold the most water with historians and scholars, as it was written very close to the time of Blackbeard's death.

Descriptions of the pirate and subsequent drawings of his image are derived from Johnsons narrative of what Blackbeard looked like back then. He writes,

> "...so our Heroe, Captain *Thatch*, assumed the Cognomen of *Black-beard*, from that large Quantity of Hair, which like a frightful Meteor, covered his whole Face, and frightn'd *America*, more than any Comet that has appear'd there a long Time. This Beard was black, which he suffered to grow of an extravagant Length; as to Breadth, it came up to his Eyes; he was accustomed to twist it with Ribbons, in small Tails, after the Manner of our Remellies Wigs, and turn them about his Ears: In time of Action, he wore a Sling over his Shoulders, with three brace of Pistols, hanging in Holsters like Bandaliers; he wore a Fur-Cap, and stuck a lighted Match on each Side, under it, which appearing on each side his Face, his Eyes naturally looking Fierce and Wild, made him altogether such a Figure, that Imagination cannot form an idea of a Fury, from Hell, to look more frightful..."

The sight of Blackbeard indeed made the most valiant of men shake in his wake. Imagine what the sight of his ghost could conjure in the deep souls of the living. It is told that he was a ruthless killer but many articles state that he never took a life unless in battle or self-defense.

The years of 1717 and 1718 were busy ones for Blackbeard. He, along with Captain Benjamin Hornigold and the gentleman pirate, Major Stede Bonnet, ran amuck along the Northern coastline of the New World. It was around this time that they took a slaver and Blackbeard renamed it the *Queen Anne's Revenge*. He turned it into a floating fortress by adding more cannons to it. There were a reported forty cannons on board. As time went on, the pirate acquired more boats and manpower to add to his army of bandits. Sometime during this span, he was said to have wed and honeymooned at the Isles of Shoals before setting out to plunder once more. He also buried treasure there according to several accounts. He left his newlywed wife to guard it until his return.

Winter forced them south where they pillaged such places as the Leeward Islands, Hispaniola, Crabb Island, and the like. In March of 1718, he took the sloop, *Adventure*. They later bottled up the Port of Charleston, South Carolina. Teach and his men took a few prizes but his main concern was for a chest of medicine. After his wish was granted, they sailed off leaving the people of Charlestown a bit poorer than before, as he also booted some gold and silver from the ships entering and leaving the harbor. Their six-day stay was most unappreciated. He sailed to North Carolina where he had the *Queen Anne's Revenge* run aground in Topsail Inlet. Another sloop raced to his aid but was wrecked along the bar as well. Some say it was on purpose to break up the company he ran with. This way he had more prize money for himself. He took a few men and boarded the sloop he had previously captured. The rest were left marooned to the elements along the Carolinas.

In mid-June of 1718, Blackbeard returned to Bath where he accepted the King's pardon for piracy. It is said he bought a home and married Mary Ormand. She is the supposed ghost that awaits his return along the Isles of Shoals.

He then sailed to Ocracoke Island. This became his favorite spot of leisure and libation. It was here that Blackbeard met his demise. While others of his consort had accepted pardons and settled down, he still chose the life of a corsair. Governor Spotswood of Virginia sent an expedition out for Blackbeard. Some traveled by land, others by sea. Lieutenant Robert Maynard caught up with Blackbeard at Teach's Hole in the Ocracoke inlet. There, a fierce battle ensued. Blackbeard fought gallantly. They both drew pistols and fired at each other. Blackbeard was wounded but continued to fight. Maynard's sword broke from the heavy clashing. As he battled with Maynard, one of Maynard's men snuck up behind the buccaneer and slashed his throat. The stunned Blackbeard kept fighting despite his wound. Maynard drew back and fired his other pistol, hitting Teach once again. The pirate still refused to cede. It would take twenty-five wounds, five of them by pistol before the legendary Blackbeard fell dead while cocking his last pistol. The rest of his men called for quarter and were duly arrested.

The lieutenant had Blackbeard's head severed from his body and hung from the bowsprit of his sloop as a trophy of his victory and warning to others who might challenge his echelon. Blackbeard's body was thrown overboard near Teach's Hole. Many say that his headless ghost still roams the water, searching for his missing head and the man who took it. Sometimes a strange glow is witnessed on the Pamlico Sound side of Ocracoke Island. This is called "Teach's Light." It is said when the light appears, you can hear a voice carried by the wind shouting, "Where's my head!" His ghost has also been seen on the beach, carrying the devilish light. It is told that the buccaneer makes his rounds looking for a victim of resembling stature to claim their head so he may enter hell with a full body. Those who witness the specter run in fear, for surely evil ends await them.

It is evidently believed that Blackbeard will not rest until he has found his head. This task could prove an eternal one, as his head was taken from Maynard's bowsprit only after seagulls had devoured its flesh. It was then sold to a wealthy merchant who, reportedly, had it dipped in silver and used it for a bowl. The skull was eventually stolen and never resurfaced again. The Ocracoke Island and surrounding area must forever endure the wraith of the ferocious pirate until such time as he can be reunited with his head, or a reasonable facsimile.

Another sight of Blackbeard's ghost is on the famous Isles of Shoals in Maine and New Hampshire. This is where he wed and spent a honeymoon. Visitors to the isles have reported seeing the countenance of the pirate on Lunging Island, facing Star Island Hotel. Prudy Crandall Randall's father bought Lunging Island in the 1920s. They set up the only home on the island. There is a spot during high tide that separates the mass into two halves. It is said that Blackbeard buried his treasure there and left his wife to guard it. It is in the black of night or the early morning mist when the glowing shade of the pirate makes his appearance. He appears to be either digging up, or burying an ethereal treasure of some sort.

A most prevalent sighting of Blackbeard's ghost happens to be on Smith and Langier Islands in the Chesapeake Bay. As the narrative goes, a man was walking by an abandoned home on Langier Island, when an echoing voice called out to him. The frightened traveler inquired the nature of the voice. The voice then told him he must reveal the location of a hidden treasure or eternally suffer torturous unrest.

The terrified man fled the scene in fear when a search revealed no human to initiate the utterances he had heard. He returned a second time a few days later but was still too sheepish to heed the words of the spirit. The man's son, who was simple in mind, had been wandering the woods near the ghostly site. One night, he returned home with two gold coins. The father then asked the boy where he acquired the gold pieces. The son told him that a misty man in a dark suit with a long beard emerged from the shadows and handed them to him. He recognized the visage immediately as that of the famous Blackbeard. The pirate ghost told him how to find the rest of the cash treasure. Unfortunately, the boy could not hold the directions in his mind long enough to reach home and relate them to his father. He could not even retrace his steps to where he met the phantom freebooter.

Thus to this day the treasures of Blackbeard remain hidden legend awaiting discovery. His ghost remains roaming the locales of his favorite places in life. His death was not the end of the golden age of piracy but only the beginning of the ageless realm of his phantom encounters that have left many a witness quaking in his wake.

Lunging Island where Blackbeard and his treasure are said to still linger.

The Dead Ship of Harpswell

The fog almost assuredly bade welcome to specters from another realm. Or, perhaps it was those phantom visitors to our side of the veil that created the haze as cover for their emergence from their world. It is not unusual for such a climate to roll into the vicinity of Harpswell, Maine. What transpired on this particular misty day is also a common incident that has reared its ethereal head for almost two centuries.

In August of 1942, America was actively in the throes of World War II. A United States Navy ship was patrolling the waters from Portland, Maine to Harpswell. An ally British ship, the *HMS Moidore*, accompanied her on her route. Suddenly, the terrifying wail of a siren shattered the serenity of Casco Bay. A couple had rowed out to Punkin Nub, one of the many islands in Casco Bay, for a picnic. An unsuspecting Homer Grimm would play a major role in one of the most fantastic ghost sightings of all time. The siren worked in alerting all patrols and personnel that an intruder had just pierced U. S. waters.

Every gun was manned and every battery became a buzzing hive of ready soldiers. This was not a drill. A call went out for the enemy ship to identify herself. There was no reply. The Navy knew the vessel was not authorized to be in the bay, and was too close to the mainland for comfort. It was at that point that the *HMS Moidore* fired upon the mysterious boat. The shell floundered slightly, striking Punkin Nub Island. The impact took off a chunk of the bluff close to where Homer Grimm and his mate were enjoying their lunch. The alerted and shaken couple gazed around the corner of the ledge where the shell hit and saw a tall ship from the previous century floating ominously at a steady clip through the breaking surf, sails full of wind.

Mr. Grimm could also see the patrolling ships bearing down on the unusual looking craft. They were close enough for him to see the men squinting to catch a glimpse of the strange ship's name. Guns rattled, sirens wailed, and all was in havoc as the Coast Guard, U. S. Navy, and British Navy swarmed in on the intruder. They all came close enough to read the name of the three-mast schooner. Homer Grimm spied it at the same time. The name on the sideboard had one word written on it—*Dash*. The *Dash* was a privateer ship that vanished one hundred and twenty eight years before this event.

The firing and sirens lulled into the void with a slow eerie trickle as the patrolling ships came to realize it was not an enemy encounter. Not an enemy from our realm, anyway. Crewmen watched in awe as the ship silently made its way through the water without a single man onboard. Not a single shell or bullet had penetrated its decks or sails. It was as if the ammunition had passed right through the phantom ship. The *Dash* then dissipated into the fog stern first, and was gone in an instant. These reputable soldiers of the sea are but a few of the many witnesses who have seen the dead ship of Harpswell. Homer Grimm is another who laid testimony that day to the supernatural return of the ghost ship. Noted locals and historians alike have concurred that the ghost ship is indeed that of the ill-fated *Dash*.

The *Dash* hailed from Porter's Landing in Freeport, Maine. James Brewer built it in 1813 for Seward, Samuel, and William Porter. She was a fast topsail schooner with a length of one hundred and three feet. Her main beam was twenty-six feet, eight inches, with a nine-foot hold depth. Her burthen weight was two hundred and twenty-two tons. She was fitted for sixteen guns. Ten of the guns were wooden models designed for intimidation as well as lightness for speed. The War of 1812 was on and the United States needed a fast ship to break and run trade that was being captured by the British fleet. The *Dash* did just that. In 1813 and 1814, she made several runs to the West Indies trading cargo.

The notoriety of the *Dash* reached President Madison. He had bigger plans for the swift schooner. On September 13, 1814, he granted a "Letter of Marque and Reprisal" to its Commander George Bacon. This allowed the ship to seize cargo and other items deemed profitable for the war efforts from enemy ships. The ship was outfitted with two eighteen-pound guns and one pivot cannon. The first voyage under her new role proved to be a great success. The second voyage was more of a triumph as not only did the crew take back a captured American sloop, but also took a British ship with a cargo of very profitable rum.

Commander John Porter took over the helm and continued the legacy. He seized fifteen prize ships in 1814 alone, leaving the *Dash* as the fearless ruler of the coast. One surprising fact about the *Dash* is that she never sustained any injury, nor did any of her crew. Her speed always beat the enemy in the end.

In January of 1815, the lucky *Dash* set sail once again along with a new privateer ship out of Portland, *Champlain*. Both were built for speed and agility. The two raced out to sea neck and neck until the *Dash* finally kicked up the juice and glided into the lead. A heavy winter gale engulfed the region and the *Champlain* wisely turned for port. The *Dash* stayed on its course. It was never seen again, in the physical sense, anyway. Captain Porter and his sixty-man crew went down with the *Dash*. Sixteen of them were from Freeport.

To this day, witnesses spy the ghost ship in Casco Bay, often defying the course of the wind as it sails silently through the waves, creating no wake from its bow and no sound from its decks. The usual creaking of the ocean going vessel is void as the eerie boat floats toward land. Legend has it that the misty ship appears when a family descendent of the original crew who disappeared in 1815 dies. It is told that the silent ghost craft makes its way into the bay. As it nears land, the deceased family member climbs aboard and joins the ghostly throng for a short but eternal journey into the afterlife. The ship then backs away into the abyss of the early evening twilight. Search through your ancestry very carefully for you might someday see the phantom *Dash* silently list to port, as the beckoning crew waves you towards the gangplank.

Harpswell's Brigand Band of Boos

Harpswell is a cherished little community that includes three large islands in Maine's Casco Bay. The three landmasses, Orr's Island, Bailey Island, and Sebacodegan are connected by a succession of bridges. The town of Harpswell consists of a narrow peninsula. Colonel Shapliegh purchased the neck and Sebacodegan Island in 1659. At the time, the Indians called the peninsula, "Merriconeag" meaning "quick carrying place." The bar was so narrow that the Indians could quickly carry their canoes over it to get from one bay to the other. Harpswell was incorporated in 1758 but was settled before that. It was also a haven for many freebooters of the East Coast.

One such place was called Pond Island. The pond has dried up and the name has been changed to Peaks Island but the ghosts still remain true to their intention. It is told how Captain Ned Lowe brought a vast treasure to the island and, with the aid of his cronies, deposited it in a secret place. Legend says that his men thought a better hiding place would be in the pond. Or, maybe they had other ideas about hoarding the gold. A collective group took the treasure and redistributed it in the pond. When Lowe found out of their deed, he became infuriated and sought their heads. They tried to regain the cache and steal away into the night. Lowe and the faithful of his crew headed them off at the pass. A bloody struggle resulted in the deaths of several crewmen. The treasure was kept safe and the rest of the corsairs stole into the moonless night.

Since then, residents of Harpswell have heard the screams and shouts of those bandits engaging in their eternal mêlée. Phantom shots ring out in the dead of night and voices from beyond permeate the silent sea air. If that is not enough, inhabitants are cursed with the spirit's ceaseless promenades around the islands. Incidents such as books flying off shelves, heavy footsteps on the floors, items taking on wings in people's homes, and even pictures lifting off walls are common to residents along the area of Harpswell. They are all blamed on the vigorous actions of the phantom buccaneers.

Other spirits may roam the islands, such as the ethereal steed that can be heard dashing down the road, yet has never been seen by any of the local folk. There was a witch that was living among the people who always stated she did not want to be buried in the Indian burial ground. When she passed, the people did exactly what she did not want. Her vengeful spirit began invading the homes of those who were responsible for her interment. Strange voices and loud rapping would wake the inhabitants up at all hours. They endured belongings mysteriously flying off shelves, accompanied by heavy footsteps around the house. Time came when they decided to carry out her original wish and bury her in the town cemetery. All supposedly became quiet once again, save for the noisy pirate phantoms, that is.

The Clara Sylvia

Phantom ships need not have to endure the centuries to gain legendary notoriety. The only major criterion is that they are either ghosts of the past, or they harbor passengers from another epoch still lingering among the decks of the doomed crafts. The *Clara Sylvia* hosts ghosts from the early twentieth century. She was a fishing boat out of Gloucester, Massachusetts but her crew hailed from another realm.

The *Clara Sylvia* was an ordinary schooner equipped with five fishing dories. Every morning she would sail to Georges Bank to reap the bounties of the sea. Once at her destination, the dories were dispatched to various locations with the fishermen crew aboard. Come nightfall, the glowing of the familiar lanterns onboard the schooner would summon the weary anglers back to her decks to bring home the day's tally of fresh fish.

One inauspicious morning, the crew noted the winds whipping up from the north and the seas becoming malevolently menacing. The ominous gray sky was a warning that a storm was on the horizon. The captain gave the command to launch the dories, but no one would oblige his order. He then demanded, under the laws of the high seas and those who sail them, that they dispatch their boats and start fishing. The crew, under oath of such laws, had no choice but to obey the captain's directive. The dories were hoisted over the side and the crew apprehensively set out among the banks to fish.

In no time, the meanest squall in memory tore through Georges Bank. The vulnerable little dinghies were tossed about the infuriated waters with no mercy. All five boats were lost in the storm and every crew-member of the *Clara Sylvia,* save for the captain and the ship's cook, went with the dories to the bottom of the ocean. They did not, however, remain there long.

When the *Clara Sylvia* returned to Gloucester with the grim news, families of the deceased pointed their vengeful fingers at the overbearing skipper. The heartless man was driven out of town never to be heard from again. The ship's cook, however, was not held accountable, as he had no power over what happened. He was as superstitious as any sailor of the seas could be. He refused to board the ship again and sought employment somewhere else. This did not deter the owners of the schooner from hiring a new crew and sending her back out to the hallowed fishing waters.

The new captain and crew set sail for the banks with the full intent of bringing home their worthy catch. Once in the abundant waters, a whole different experience awaited them. Each night they heard the sounds of knives cutting bait below decks. When the uneasy new crew went below to check out the ethereal noises, there was not a soul found. The noises continued through the bowers of the eerie nights. The fishermen knew it was the old crew, come back to resume their tasks of baiting their hooks and readying for the next day; a day that would last forever for the ghostly crew.

As if the ghostly chopping was not enough to turn a hardened seamen's legs to jelly, each night after the demise of the mysterious hewing from below decks, another chilling occurrence would render them utterly unnerved. The original ill-fated crew took pleasure in the smoking of their favorite pipes, cigars, and cigarettes after a day of angling in the ocean. Each night, they would appear on the deck in the same spot they did in life, reclining with their tobaccos along the railing of the bow. The ghastly glow of the countenances was too much for the present crew to behold. They shied clear from the top deck after dark. But there was still the chopping sound below. The ominous echo of the cleavers reverberated throughout the ship as they struck the old cutting board. This, their senses could not evade. When the *Clara Sylvia* made port, the captain and crew made tracks for the driest land possible, never looking back at the haunted vessel.

The owners of the schooner soon found another brave crew. They took the *Clara Sylvia* to another part of the sea to fish but the phantom crew still went about their routine on the cursed craft. It became evident that the haunted schooner was taboo to all the sailors of the region. Not even the most fearless farer of the briny would dare set sail on the ghost ship. The vessel was no longer in the control of the living. She now belonged to the world of the beyond.

The owners thought by sending her to Nova Scotia, the spirits aboard would leave the ship once in unfamiliar grounds. They were dead wrong. The phantom crew made their vigil as timely as ever. No one would go below after dark once the unearthly cutting started. Then, the living crew would have to avert their eyes as the wraiths were summoned upon the top deck for their eternal retreat from their duties. The schooner truly became a ghost ship. No one can say for sure what happened to the *Clara Sylvia*. She never returned to Gloucester and no questions arose of her fate. Perhaps she just faded into the void between the living and the dead, and is now roaming among those shadows that sailors see in the distance when the moon is full, and the schools of fish are ripe for the shoalers. Both, living or otherwise…

Monument surrounded by plaques with the names of the thousands of
Gloucester fishermen who met their fate at sea.

The City of Columbus

This next account concerns two kinds of haunting incidents. One was a premonition and the other, a watchful phantom. This story has come up several times while visiting Cape Cod in Massachusetts. The beginning hails out of New Market, New Hampshire. Sounds a bit confusing? Read on and the final moment's accounts of the *City of Columbus* will shed light on the tale that sits before the inquisitive.

The *City of Columbus* was a two thousand ton steamship commanded by Captain Schuyler Wright. The two hundred and seventy foot vessel left Boston on January 17, 1884, bound for ports in Georgia and Florida. The typical New England frigidity had gripped the region as temperatures plummeted. The one hundred and thirty-two people aboard were already dreaming of the warm coastal air that pervaded in the southern part of the country.

Soon the steamer passed into the Vineyard Sound just off the shores of Cape Cod. For reasons unknown, the captain was at the brink of collapse from exhaustion. He figured a small nap would do him a world of good. He relinquished the helm to his first mate and scurried below for a quick repose. Sometime between that moment and what transpired next aboard the ship, a gent named Nathaniel Bunker in New Market, New Hampshire, woke with a terrible start. It was a nightmare so vivid, so horrible, that he hastily summoned his best friends to his door. At that point he told them of his dreadful premonition.

There he was, standing on a high bluff overlooking the ocean, when a steam ship came into view. At first all seemed tranquil. Then, a large crunching sound shattered the serenity of the moment as the ship hit something, causing it to break up in the water. He watched helplessly from the cliffs as the passengers struggled in vain to save themselves in the freezing waters below. It was at that moment he could see his new son-in-law, Louis Chase, desperately fighting to hoist a woman into a lifeboat. The woman was Nathaniel's daughter and Louis's bride. In an instant a great wave overcame the lifeboat and all were swept into the sea, vanishing under the raging surf.

The fact was that Nathaniel's daughter had indeed married Louis Chase two days previously. They set out for Boston where they boarded the *City of Columbus* to celebrate their honeymoon in the south. His friends tried to convince him that it was just a bad dream brought on by the stressful events of the wedding and his daughter's new sovereignty. Mr. Bunker knew the nightmare was too vivid to be a product of nothing else but a portent of bad omen.

His fears were confirmed when news reached his door of the disaster aboard the *City of Columbus*. The ship had struck an outcropping of rocks called

"Devil's Bridge." The first mate and night watch were not quick enough in their duty to see the marker buoy that warned mariners of the navigational hazard. The vessel plowed straight into the rocks. The captain immediately came on deck and reversed the ship away from the ledge, thus settling the damaged boat in deep waters where it sank quickly, taking one hundred and three passengers to their doom. Two of those travelers were Nathaniel's daughter and son-in-law. Those who clung to the rigging froze to death in the icy hours that followed. It took eight hours for boats to brave the waters of the sound. Indians from Gay Head who selflessly saved twenty-nine people that night manned them. Among the survivors, only one child was saved. He was twelve-year-old George Farnsworth. Had Schuyler Wright chose to stay on the bar, or push forward, the boat would have come to rest in shallow water and all aboard would have been spared.

Schuyler Wright was discharged as a ship master and left his native home in Wareham to work on Georgia docks the rest of his life. Nathaniel Bunker's nightmare had foretold a terrible disaster that left him broken in heart and soul. Schuyler Wright soon passed away and his forlorn spirit was later seen by the Gay Head Indians on the cliffs of Devil's Bridge waving a sign of warning to all ships passing by. To this day, mariners navigating the rocky outcropping can behold the wraith eternally trying to atone for his fatal error that January night back in 1884.

So, there it is. The tale of two supernatural occurrences linked to one tragedy among the many that have transpired along the coast of New England. At least there is comfort in knowing that there is an eternal watcher to guide the unwary past the danger known as Devil's Bridge. Even if it came about at such a terrible cost.

Black Bart and the Turnip Field

Pirates by trade are not prone to farming. Their ships are not land-going vessels either. These two facts are quite logical. If so, then why, or how, did the famous pirate Black Bart and his ship once end up in a turnip patch? Read on and enjoy this next account of the most dashing corsair known throughout history.

Bartholomew Roberts was quite a figure in the world of the freebooters. He was born in 1682, in what is now Little Newcastle in Pembrokeshire, Wales. His first name was John but he changed it to Bartholomew for unknown reasons. He was a seafarer from his early teens. He sailed with Captain Davis on a mission to kidnap the governor of the Isles of Princes. The governor found out and ambushed Davis as he made shore.

Roberts became captain by vote. His bravery and outspoken style had already made its mark on his career to be. He first enacted revenge upon the village where his captain was killed, then set course into the full-blown life of a pirate. His dashing style of dress was in direct contrast to that of a typical pirate. He wore bright colored breeches and waistcoats. His pistols usually hung from sashes of silk, and he adorned his hat with a large feather. He was quite the spectacle among the pirate world. He was also the most successful buccaneer by far.

From 1719 to 1722, it is reported that Black Bart took over four hundred and fifty ships. He truly admired bravery in the enemy. He once held great ire towards the crews of twenty-two ships when they fled their boats for the mainland upon his arrival. He relentlessly taunted them, calling for them to turn and fight like sailors, not run like dogs. He also abhorred drunkenness while out at sea. He knew a ship could be spied at any moment. It was then dire necessity for his men to be sober and ready for battle. His articles of law aboard his ship were quite straightforward:

1. Every man shall have an equal vote in affairs of moment. He shall have an equal title to the fresh provisions or strong liquors at any time seized, and shall use them at pleasure unless a scarcity may make it necessary for the common good that a retrenchment may be voted.

2. Every man shall be called fairly in turn by the list on board of prizes, because over and above their proper share, they are allowed a shift of clothes. But if they defraud the company to the value of even one dollar in plate, jewels or money, they shall be marooned. If any man rob another he shall have his nose and ears slit, and be put ashore where he shall be sure to encounter hardships.

3. None shall game for money either with dice or cards.

4. The lights and candles should be put out at eight at night, and if any of the crew desire to drink after that hour they shall sit upon the open deck without lights.

5. Each man shall keep his piece, cutlass and pistols at all times clean and ready for action.

6. No boy or woman to be allowed amongst them. If any man shall be found seducing any of the latter sex and carrying her to sea in disguise he shall suffer death.

7. He that shall desert the ship or his quarters in time of battle shall be punished by death or marooning.

8. None shall strike another on board the ship, but every man's quarrel shall be ended on shore by sword or pistol in this manner. At the word of command from the quartermaster, each man being previously placed back to back, shall turn and fire immediately. If any man do not, the quartermaster shall knock the piece out of his hand. If both miss their aim they shall take to their cutlasses, and he that draweth first blood shall be declared the victor.

9. No man shall talk of breaking up their way of living till each has a share of 1,000. Every man who shall become a cripple or lose a limb in the service shall have 800 pieces of eight from the common stock and for lesser hurts proportionately.

10. The captain and the quartermaster shall each receive two shares of a prize, the master gunner and boatswain, one and one half shares, all other officers one and one quarter, and private gentlemen of fortune one share each.

11. The musicians shall have rest on the Sabbath Day only by right. On all other days by favor only.

Some say he was a tea-totaler but it is likely he was prone to stay sober during the patrol portions of his exploits. This would explain his success and longetivity compared to his contemporaries. Black Bart finally met his fate in February of 1722. On February 5, 1722, the HMS *Swallow* entered Cape Lopez. The *Royal Fortune, Ranger,* and *Little Ranger* were moored there. As the

Swallow veered to avoid a sandbar, Commander James Skyrme of the *Ranger* thought the ship was turning tail and running. He set out after the vessel. Imagine his surprise when the gun ports flew open and he realized it was a British man of war. Ten of his men were killed and Skyrme lost his leg to a cannonball.

On February 10th, the *Swallow* returned to see the *Royal Fortune* under the command of Bartolomew Roberts still in port. Roberts had taken the *Neptune* on the previous day, and being full of liquor, his crew made much mirth. They were not prepared for what was about to ensue. A deserter from the British man of war recognized the craft and rushed below to warn Roberts, who was having breakfast with the captain of the *Neptune*. He informed Roberts that the *Swallow* sailed best upon the wind with her sails and trim. If the *Royal Fortune* needed to break away from the British ship, she could go before the wind. Thus, a plan and preparations for battle were made.

Roberts dressed for battle in his finest attire. Crimsom breeches and waistcoat, a gold chain with a diamond cross about his neck, and a sash of silk brandishing two pistols. To top off his gallant wardrobe, he wore a feather of bright red in his cap. Armed with sword in hand, he commanded his men to fight. He expected to sail past the great warship with one broadside confrontation but the helmsman either erred in his wind calculation, or the wind itself changed course. Either way, the *Royal Fortune* could not get past the *Swallow* which delivered several blows to the pirate ship.

Roberts was killed by grapeshot cannon fire when it struck him in the throat. Grapeshot fire consisted of anything from glass to rocks or slugs packed in canvass. It acted much like the rounds from a shotgun. The crew immediately threw him overboard. He had repeatedly directed his men to do just that, should he ever succumb to the throes of battle. This was not the end of the pirate according to legend. We do know the history of his life. What about the afterlife?

As stated before, there is a story by Richard Middleton, published after his death in 1911, on the ghost of Black Bart that is quite amusing. It is from the book, *The Ghost Ship, and Other Stories*. I will present a quick summary of the tale for the reader to get the idea of just how a ghost can effect the lives of a community.

After a storm in Portland, England, a farmer notices that there is a ship in his turnip field. Why would a ship be in a field fifty miles from the ocean? When the farmer inquires about the mysterious vessel, he comes face to face with none other than Black Bart. The farmer knows that the corsair has been dead for almost three hundred years yet he still asks counsel with the ghost.

The farmer tells him the ship has ruined some of his crops, and the apologetic Roberts hands him a very expensive piece of jewelry in compensation for his loss. Soon the other ghosts in town start cohorting with the phantom pirate and his crew. The ghostly parties run through the night. Before long, the townspeople become worried over their familiar friends from the other side. They are staying up way too late and wandering their haunts rather sluggishly. The village leaders dispatch to the ship where they charge Roberts with creating a nuisance among the spirits of their community. He tells them he has no control over their afterlives and offers the living some of the finest rum they ever consumed.

This seems to appease their anger long enough to see the pirate ship, and some of the resident ghosts, gone one morning. The people of the village took their ghosts quite seriously and felt a loss over the migration of those who checked out with the wraith of Black Bart. Still, the townsfolk went on their way with their lives, and afterlives and all ended well.

Is this tale too far fetched? As for its validity, I cannot say either yay or nay. But, do keep in mind the many things that were once a product of unreachable science fiction when we were children. I say this of course as I glance over at someone's camera/computer/I-pod/camcorder/cell phone ringing.

The Ghostly Woman's Warning of the Usk

When the *Usk* left port in February of 1863, no one ever imagined what would transpire over the next few months. She sailed from Cardiff, Wales, headed for Huacho, Peru laden with coal and iron for trade in the West Indies. The journey was long and rough. Unexpected storms delayed the ship's otherwise profitable venture. Captain Richard Brown kept the men and the ship on course as best as he could, but one moment in time would completely change that.

Captain Brown was standing on the quarterdeck looking out over the sea towards Cape Horn, which loomed somewhere in the distant twilight. He was worried about the setbacks the voyage had endured, and wondered what was in store for him next. Suddenly, something moved out of the corner of his eye. Among the sails, there appeared a woman, wearing the most brilliant white veils. The stunned captain ogled in disbelief at the apparition that had just materialized out of nowhere. She beckoned him forth with a slow wave of her ghostly upper limb. As he motioned towards the wraith, she floated towards him with a portentous look about her ethereal visage.

"You must turn back," she told him. "Go immediately back to where you came, or you will surely suffer the destruction of your ship and crew, as well as yourself! Tell them I have ordained it!" The wraith then slowly evaporated into the emerging fog and was gone in an instant.

Captain Brown was very shook up over this omen and ordered the crew on deck. "We must turn back at once. I know we have come far, and our destination is at hand but I have been given dire orders to retreat back to Cardiff at once!" He then retired to his cabin where the first mate and a few crewmen followed.

Once below, the first mate began to challenge the commander's orders. It was far too unreasonable to relinquish such a trip to some folly. Captain Brown made one more demand for the ship's new course to be charted, due Northeast. When the first mate became rebellious, he had him put in irons and held in the brig. Anyone else who dare challenge the bold decision to return to Cardiff would suffer the same fate. The crew knew that something had indisputably spooked their captain.

Soon the truth came out about the phantom woman who appeared on the deck and the crew began to doubt their commander's sanity. When the ship made port in the British Isles, the crew hastily fled the *Usk,* never looking back. Captain Brown called counsel with the owners of the vessel and explained the extraordinary circumstances that hailed his abrupt return. The owners were outraged by his claims and had him imprisoned for insubordination of duty, as well as the expenses rendered for the failed business venture.

A hearing was held and the crew testified that the captain acted quite irrationally in his undertaking of the journey. He was stripped of his papers to command a vessel and was ridiculed for his testimony. A new captain was put in command of the *Usk* but no crew would board her. The accounts of the woman's ghost were so stunning that the local sailors feared it was an omen of sure disaster. Even the old crew who helped in the demise of the captain's vocation became fearful of the premonition that Richard Brown swore he had witnessed.

Eventually a crew of outsiders were brought in to sail the *Usk* to Huacho. The owners were comforted with the thought that they would finally reap from their predicament. Four months later, they were shocked when news of the *Usk* reached their desk. The ship met with a most disastrous fate when a candle in the storeroom supposedly set fire to some cloth. The flames spread faster than they could be quenched. The ship burned and sank with all aboard. They labeled it as an accident, but the sailors of Cardiff knew better. They buzzed about the captain who listened to the warnings given by the ghostly woman. It was known that the new commander of the *Usk* was not prone to believe in such forecasts of ill fate. Perhaps the new skipper should have listened, when the woman in white appeared on the deck just before the flames rose from the depths below to claim them.

The Sagunto, Conception, and Spanish Graves

The nature of this next chronicle recruits itself into this tome chiefly on the merits of historical enigma. The fact that there are supernatural happenings involved goes without saying. There has been a veil of vagueness that has impaired the facts regarding the wreck of a Spanish ship near Smuttynose Island in 1813. Legend and folklore in both rhyme and reason have painted quite a scene on the canvas of poetic license. No one knows for sure what the real truth is. Perhaps it is under the rocky soil of Smuttynose. It also may rest deep within the waters of the Isles of Shoals, waiting for discovery. Until then, here is what is known and told about the haunted ship and graves.

The Isles of Shoals are among the most intriguing places to visit anywhere. Literary greats such as Hawthorne, Thoreau, Whittier, Snow, and lifetime resident Celia Thaxter wrote of the incredible allure the rocky outcroppings possess. But, do not be fooled by the beauty and illustrious history that awaits the adventurer, for there is another side to the Isles of Shoals that can steal the bravado from the sternest of souls. On the night of January 14, 1813, that side reared its wrath in the form of a full-blown squall that reigned upon the region.

Sam Haley Jr. was the sole occupant of Smuttynose. He kept a candle aglow at night to warn mariners of the treachery the isles can bestow upon wayward ships. He knew the dim light was no match for the blinding snow that whipped across the land and sea, yet habit compelled him to carry out his conviction. He soon found himself tired from the day's tarry of securing his possessions from the icy grip of the blizzard. He fell into a restful sleep. So restful was his slumber, he was never stirred by the loud crash of a vessel on the Cedar Island ledge just off Smuttynose.

The ship, a four hundred ton galleon with twenty-eight men aboard had picked up some dried cod from the Portsmouth port and was headed back to Spain with other cargo such as raisins, almonds, and cloth. Her captain, Don Juan Coxava decided to brave the elements and sail out of the blizzard. This was not to be. As the ship broke up, the sailors tried to make it to the islands. Some saw the faint glow of Haley's candle in the distance. Others were not so fortunate, as the storm and waves took them to their watery graves.

Sam Haley arose the next morning and looked out his window to find the most ghastly sight. The frozen bodies of three men lay outside his window. One man had almost made it to the front door before collapsing on the wall from exhaustion. From there the elements had taken over. The other two were a little further from the home. Sam Haley could not believe he slept through the whole ordeal. As he searched the shore, more bodies washed ashore along with the wreckage of the ship and its cargo. He then took the sailors and buried them in a mass grave near the family plot. From there it is said that he fashioned crude headstones, eventually fourteen in all, and gave them proper burial. As to the ship, it is said that the vessel was the *Sagunto,* but later records show the *Sagunto* made it safely to Newport and waited out the storm. Sam Haley told a Massachusetts court that the wreck was that of the *Conception* out of Cadiz, Spain.

For weeks after, wreckage from the ship floated to shore along the eastern side of Smuttynose. It is reported that one of the crew was found six months later in the brush near the water's edge. The legend of the wreck and its fated crew were immortalized in the poems of Portsmouth native James Kennard Jr., and Isles of Shoals inhabitant Celia Thaxter. The former appeared in 1847, while the latter surfaced in 1865. The first poem tells of the horrible disaster and the fate of the men while the second, by Thaxter, relates to the feelings she exudes after seeing their all but forgotten graves. It appears they may have been forgotten over time but are attempting to keep the legacy alive.

Ghosts of the Spanish sailors have been seen on the island, which is part of Maine. Researchers have found what appear to be fourteen headstones and footstones rambling among the overgrowth. Their studies showed that the topsoil on the rocky island was only about one foot deep. If they were buried, it can be assumed that many boulders were placed over their graves to protect them from the elements. Perhaps they roam the island trying to set the story of their fate straight. It could be that they are at unrest due to the shabby conditions of their burial. That is no fault of Haley. It is the make up of the isle itself.

Maybe they come from the void to hail their ship, the *Conception*. It is told by many that one of the phantom vessels of the isles is the Spanish craft that met with an untimely eternal rest under the waters of the isles. Some say it returns on the anniversary of the wreck to claim its crew and sail back home. Perhaps the sailors rise from their timeless sleep in wait of the galleon that sailed them into eternity and legend. They are forever roaming among the shores of Smuttynose, hoping for a glimpse of the misty ship to appear on the horizon.

Maybe then they can be at peace. Celia Thaxter tells of how their families await, never knowing truly, where their loved ones repose in their desolate graves. Did she know something that we don't?

The Alice Marr

The story of the *Alice Marr* was born of beauty, love, and tragedy. Gloucester seems to have an awesome array of ghost ships floating its waters. Each has a different tale to tell of the reason they linger in eternity's ebb and tide. The *Alice Marr* is a short but quaint tale.

Alice Marr was a very beautiful woman. Her father was a sea captain and it seemed only fitting that she would follow into that life when the proper suitor struck her fancy. Being of handsome countenance, every man far and near came courting on Alice. They tried every form of flattery to entice her to be their bride. One man, John Ackman found favor in her when he moored his ship close to port and there on the side, read her name, *Alice Marr.*

This act of devotion won her over. The sea captain's daughter was to marry another captain of the ship bearing her name. But first he had but one more important fishing trip to set sail on before they wed. Ackman proudly sailed out of Gloucester eagerly wanting to return and marry.

Months passed without a word from the *Alice Marr.* Soon a year had bore down on the town with no news as to the fate of the ship bearing the woman's name. All knew that she was surely lost at sea. Then one day someone came with reports that the *Alice Marr* lay just over the horizon. A group of sailors dispatched boats to greet the ship but as they neared the vessel, it grew further away. For some strange reason, they could not shorten the distance between them and the *Alice Marr.* They called to the skipper but saw no man aboard. Suddenly, the ship just vanished before their eyes.

The men came back with their account of the eerie incident, and all knew that the ship and her crew were now a part of the other side of life. The heartbroken Alice Marr never married. She spent the rest of her life wandering the shore looking for a glimpse of the boat that bore her name. E. Norman Gunnison put the legend to verse, relating the story of the ghost ship and the lost love. Every New Year's Eve, The *Alice Marr* can be seen silently gliding over the water, her bow making no break among the surf. As she nears the port, the witnesses will see the phantom ship disappear into the twilight. It is assumed that the ship met her fate on that day way back when. All is once again serene until the next year when she returns in despair, hoping to make it to port and fulfill the endless promise of love and marriage.

The Bay of Fundy's Phantom Freebooter

There is a place called Cape Forchu in Nova Scotia, just east of the Gulf of Maine. There, in the Fundy Bay, sits a rocky ledge known as the Roaring Bull. To mariners, the outcropping has been a navigational haunt for centuries. There is another haunt that is said to cast a shadow on the waters as well. That is the ghostly galleon of a wicked pirate by the name of Black Bartelmy.

Bartelmy met his end at Cape Forchu when his ship, bursting over the sides with plunder, became victim to the merciless bay fog and thrashing waters. The waves drove his galleon into the ledges of the Roaring Bull with such vigor; it split the hull wide open. The crew was forced to take as much treasure as possible and abandon ship. It is told that Black Bartelmy and his first mate then killed the crew, one by one, and took the treasure to an undisclosed cave for hiding. They loaded the cache into the crevice, then sealed it with boulders.

As the first mate finished this task, Bartelmy, being the murderous rogue he was, thrust his cutlass into his partner, killing him on the spot. It is then told that Bartelmy wandered off to find a town and fell into quicksand where he perished. As he took his last breath, he shouted to the heavens, swearing he would return. The area is actually a hotbed of old volcanoes. His cause of demise is a matter of conjecture but the next accounts are not.

Many years later, 1839 to be exact, a lighthouse was commissioned to look over the Bay of Fundy. The light is now referred to as the "Old Yarmouth Light." The first keepers were the Fox family. They tended the beacon from 1839 to 1874. The light was actually first lit on January 15, 1840. Not long after, the keeper saw a distress signal coming from the vicinity of the Roaring Bull. He quickly gathered a rescue team and rowed out to the scene. They were not prepared for what awaited them. There, in the misty fog of the rocky ledge, emerged a galleon of the old world. Its sails tattered by centuries of wind, and its sides rotted and falling apart. On board was a lone man standing among vast chests of gold and jewels. The rescuers were certain that the vision before them was that of a ghost ship. It silently moved by them with the corsair on board waving his cutlass. They remembered the story of Black Bartelmy and realized the evil man had come back. Suddenly, a great wave overcame the rescue boat and the men's vision was lost for a moment. In that spec of time, the galleon had vanished from their sight. They rowed back to the light in disbelief.

Since then, there are many tales of the distress signal that lures rescue crews to the Roaring Bull, only to come face to face with the brutal buccaneer and his hellish galleon. The vessel then vanishes with the evil guffaw of Black Bartelmy still echoing over the surf. The light has been automated since 1993 and a light buoy sits as a warning near the Roaring Bull. The light and keeper's quarters are now a museum open from April to October, 9 am to 9 pm. No one can say if the ghostly galleon has made its vigil over the recent few years. Many of the old salts of the bay area say the story is as real as the white stubble on their faces.

Whether the story is true, or just embellishments from the works of M. V. Marshall and Jeffery Farnol, who wrote ballads and stories of Black Bartelmy and his treasure, is a matter you must decide for yourself. Pay a visit to the light and wait until the sun descends below the horizon. Perhaps you will see a distress signal in the distance. It could be a call for help, or, it could be something else.

The Squando

Some ships cannot escape their curses, no matter where they sail. The *Squando* was one such boat that moved from coast to coast with a most foul entity aboard, forever bringing death and destruction to those who sailed her.

In 1889, the first mate of the ship was found murdered in his cabin. His head had been cut off. The captain and his wife were arrested for the crime and found guilty. It seems the first mate was always arguing with the captain's wife. The couple put an end to the constant bickering by taking off the man's head with an axe. The ship was then transferred from San Francisco to South America but evil followed, as well.

The new crew mutinied and cut off the captain's head. There seemed to be a pattern arising. The owners took her back to the West Coast and hired yet another crew. They were unaware of the previous tragedies aboard the boat, but were to soon become part of the ship's legacy. On route to the West Indies, the captain mysteriously died. Once in the Indies, a new captain was procured. He too succumbed to a strange death. The *Squando* reached port in Bathhurst, New Brunswick, just north of the New England border where the crew hastily abandoned ship. There were reports of ghostly figures roaming around on the ship and eerie voices that saturated the night air, waking the sailors with a trembling start.

The ship sat at port with no men to sail her. The owners called the Canadian Consul for protection of the haunted vessel. Two men were hired to stay aboard the boat to keep thieves from stealing its cargo. John LeClerc and Haley Robinson took their job seriously, but fled in panic several days later. They reported that they heard voices in the cabins. When they would investigate, the rooms were void of any physical being. Cold hands would grab them, and bed sheets were pulled from them as they slept. Items also took on wings in the cabin they bunked in. A spike reportedly flew across the room and imbedded itself in the floor between LeClec's legs. One night, all the lanterns onboard went out in an instant. Haley Robinson even saw the apparition of a headless sailor on the quarterdeck.

Dock workers were later hired to remove the cargo from the cursed ship. As they entered the hold, spikes flew at them just missing their heads while voices screeched out of the darkness. They flew from the scene never looking back. Later they all told the same story of how the incident left them unnerved. No one would ever board the ghostly ship again. It actually sat docked in the same spot until it rotted and sank, still laden with cargo.

Now, when the night gets quiet, the sounds from below still rise to remind those who might want to adventure out to the remains of the *Squando*, it is best to leave the ghosts to their own.

Plymouth's Mystery Ship and Burial Hill

Every year, multitudes of tourists flock to Plymouth Rock to pay homage to the celebrated birthplace of America. The area is a scenic symphony for the senses. There is a picturesque wonder that is not always visible. It sits just beyond the memorial rock. It is the reported wreck of the *General Arnold*. It is said that the ship was cursed to suffer its horrific fate due to the name she was given. But there is a mystery that shrouds its actual whereabouts. The crew is interred up on Burial Hill in Plymouth in a mass grave. Even the story behind that is rather strange. Their ghosts do not rest, especially one in particular. Lets start from the beginning and let you, the reader become the final judge of this whole conundrum. From this point on the ship will be referred to as the "G" out of respect for the crew and their superstitions.

Christmas, 1778, The Revolutionary War was in full throttle and the cold was more than one could stand. The *Revenge* and the "G" set sail for the Carolinas. The "G" was stocked with supplies and troops to help the colonial militias in the south keep the British from separating the territories. Captain James Magee was more than ready to fight the British whom he loathed so much from battles in his homeland of Ireland.

As the two ships rounded Cape Cod, the usual un-expected Northeast winds turned malevolent. Before long they were in blizzard conditions. The *Revenge* sat out the storm in Cape Cod Harbor while the "G" sought the calmer waters of Plymouth, just past Gurnet Point Light. They dropped anchor and furled the sails, but the storm was too intense. The ship began sliding towards land. Even attempts to weigh the hull with their cannons failed. When the anchor lines broke, the brig crashed into what is known as White Flat. She began to take on water until the main deck was knee deep in the icy brine. Within hours, some of the men had already frozen to death in the snow and ice drifts that covered the deck. A few were washed overboard by the relentless surf. Others had found a cargo of liquor in the hold and began drinking it to stay warm. Captain Magee suggested that they soak their feet and hands with it to prevent frostbite, but only a few resorted to that use of the libation.

The next morning, the scene was even more grim. More had succumbed to the elements. Many froze stiff in the position they were either standing or sitting in. The ship's dory was put into the water with a few of the soldiers in an attempt to make land, but they disappeared and were never seen again. Captain Magee saw a break in the storm and fired a signal flare towards the mainland. The people of Plymouth saw the signal but could not reach the boat in the restless waves and ice floes.

Thinking quickly, they began to build a causeway to the marooned ship by packing the ice and snow. All the while Captain Magee made his men walk briskly to keep their circulation going. The citizens of Plymouth worked around the clock until they finally reached the boat. It was an incredible undertaking. On the morning of December 28th, they finally reached the vessel. Scores of dead bodies were strewn about the decks, all frozen. Some were piled up to keep the surviving protected from the brutal winds. The dead were brought to the courthouse, while the living were transported to area homes for the painful process of thawing out.

There were those that were presumed dead, as one young man who could not move. As the rescuers began to tie him to be thrown over the side, then dragged to the ice road where a sled awaited to carry the dead, he began blinking his eyes rapidly, and he was saved from being thrown into the water for passage back to the mainland. Once all the bodies were brought to shore, the dead were buried in a mass grave on Burial Hill. Some were frozen together as they had huddled trying to stay warm. Others could not be straightened out and were buried in their posture at the time of their demise.

Some of the survivors died over the next few days. Sixty-six men were buried up on the hill. Captain Magee never suffered frostbite but lived with a far worse infliction, the consequence of his decision. He helped the twenty-four surviving passengers with his own wages until his early death in 1801 at the age of fifty-one years. Although he had made a fair amount of money for a decent burial, he had requested that he be buried in the mass grave along with his men on Burial Hill. This was done. As for the ship, the story continues.

There are two camps in this saga. One camp claims that the ship sank and was found in 1976, when a breakwater changed the tide flow, washing the sand from a seventy-five foot section of the buried hull. Charles

Sanderson III was one of the people who discovered the wreck. He, along with other "discoverers" put a claim on the site. The Pilgrim Society of Plymouth was another that reportedly discovered the wreck. They soon withdrew their claim, citing the ship in the harbor was nothing more than a sunken coal barge. They produced evidence in documentation supporting their claim.

According to the society, the ship got stuck in the ice. Still in good condition, it was repaired and re-rigged, then sent out once again. It was later captured by the British and renamed. From there, it became a private merchant ship. Its whereabouts at that point are unknown. Mr. Sanderson became sole owner of a coal barge. But did he have a useless old boat or the real deal?

Tireless dives to the site by Sanderson and his son, along with others, proved fruitful. They began to find colonial mess kits, scabbards, bowls, and bottles. They even found cannonballs and other items suggesting that the ship was indeed the famous warship. A few items had initials carved in them. The initials matched those of crewmembers aboard the "G" and it appeared that Sanderson had the last laugh. A documentary on the ship and its fate was released taking the side that insists the vessel was salvaged and repaired. Although the items found at the site were of military stature, no one is sure if the boat there is the "G." So now there are two sides stating two different things. What did happen to the ship? Is it somewhere else, or did it really sink in Plymouth Harbor?

Let it also be mentioned that the ghosts of the heroic and brave crew are among those that haunt Burial Hill. There are reports that figures in colonial army garb have been seen both in the cemetery, and the antique store just across the street. Main Street Antiques may house some of the clues as to why they are restless. It could also be a favorite wandering place, as the store is tenant to other remnants of the past, as well. Could it be the relentless question surrounding their ship's actual fate? Are they looking for the boat, or are they trying to tell someone that they know what became of the vessel that no one ever called by name again? It could be none of the above. Perhaps they are not at peace while the subject remains unsolved. Perhaps they are still at unrest over their term of demise.

The entrance to Burial Hill in Plymouth.

Looking out from Plymouth Rock into the harbor where the cursed ship is reported to still remain.

Maybe the unfortunate ship is on the other side as well, sailing into the vast void, trying to shed the fate that sealed its name and destiny. It could easily be one of the many unknown misty ships that can be seen silently listing past unsuspecting wayfarers before vanishing in the mysterious but alluring sea.

One more interesting note is that General Benedict Arnold is claimed to have become a traitor to the American people when he attended a Tory party on Christmas Eve, 1778. Was it coincidence or curse?

The 1749 Courthouse where the frozen bodies were taken. It is now a museum.

Mass grave on Burial Hill of the brave soldiers who perished December 1778 while en route to fight for freedom. Captain Magee would later be interred here with his men.

Joshua Slocum's Ethereal Helmsman

The life of Captain Joshua Slocum was, to say the least, quite adventurous. He was born near the Bay of Fundy, Nova Scotia on February 20, 1844. At age fourteen, he ran away from home to become a cook on a schooner. He soon returned, but left for good two years later at the age of sixteen. He knew then that the sea was his life.

In 1869, he obtained his first command of a ship sailing from San Francisco, California to ports in Japan, China, Australia, and the Spice Islands. He married his first wife in Sydney, Australia on January 31, 1871. After thirteen years of sailing to the aforementioned places, he left in 1882 to command and own the ship, *Northern Light*. In 1884, he sold the *Northern Light* and bought the bark, *Aquidneck*. Unfortunately, his wife died that same year and was buried in Buenos Aries.

In 1886, he married Henrietta Elliot. The *Aquidneck* made several voyages but was wrecked on a sandbar off the coast of Brazil in 1887. This did nothing to deter the adventurer/captain/commander. He then sailed a thirty-five foot canoe, the *Liberdade*, with his wife, his youngest son, Garfield, and his oldest son, Victor five thousand miles to Washington D. C. where the canoe was set to join the elite artifacts of the Smithsonian Institute. Somewhere along the way, the boat was put into storage and vanished from history.

In 1892, Captain Eben Pierce offered Slocum a boat that had been sitting in a field in Fairhaven, Massachusetts. It was a thirty-seven foot oyster sloop that would go from field, to maritime, then haunted history. Its name was the *Spray*. She was repaired, and on April 24, 1895, Joshua Slocum left Boston Harbor to embark on the first solo voyage around the world. It was not long into the voyage that Captain Slocum would become a believer in the supernatural.

His records put him in Gibraltar around August 25, 1895. It was somewhere between there and the Azores that a terrible squall hit the area. At the same time, Slocum came down with immense stomach pains. They were so severe that he actually left his duty of bringing in the sails and fell below in great pain. At some point, he realized that the ship, full of sail in the storm, was destined to wreck. As he struggled to the deck, he saw a man at the helm guiding the ship. He became fearful that he had just been boarded by pirates and surely would suffer at their hand. The strange man was dressed in very old-fashioned sailing clothes with a red cap. The man then spoke to him, relating that he was the helmsman of the *Pinta*, one of the ships in Columbus's party. He yelled to Slocum that he must catch up with the *Pinta*, and therefore needed more sail. Slocum listened with great confusion as the man told him to rest. The sailor went on to relate how Slocum had gotten a bad ache from mixing the plums with cheese. Slocum went below again thinking it a bad dream.

Time went by and Joshua Slocum went back on deck to find the sailor gone. To his astonishment, the ship was still on perfect course, despite the raging storm that should have wrecked the boat; no less bring it out of its charted route. That night he had a dream. The sailor returned to him thanking him for staying below and getting well enough to return to the helm. He also, as Slocum reported, stated that he would like to accompany such a brave man on more adventures. Then the phantom sailor was gone in a whisp.

Needless to say, Captain Joshua Slocum made history as he entered Newport Harbor on June 27, 1898. He had successfully sailed around the world, but was he truly alone? The *Spray* came to port in Fairhaven on July 3, 1898, and from there Captain Slocum wrote about his fantastic journey in his book, *Sailing Alone Around the World*.

It was published in 1900 and is still in print. In the book, he tells of his supernatural experience with a hand from the other side. Some say it was delirium that caused the apparition. Others claim that Slocum himself, a man of great fortitude, somehow managed to unconsciously steer his vessel safely through the storm. One thing is for certain; the voyage was certainly incredible enough where such an account did not need to be made up. We must take his word that something happened out there. Something quite extraordinary kept Slocum from meeting his maker.

In 1902, the now famous Joshua Slocum settled into a house on Martha's Vineyard with his family. They still sailed south every winter, returning to New England for the summer. On November 14, 1909, at the age of sixty-five, Joshua Slocum and the *Spray* sailed into eternity. He left Vineyard Haven for a voyage to South America and was never seen or heard from again. It is quite a lamentable ending to a great man's life. Maybe now he also is at helms, helping troubled navigators past imminent doom. One would certainly want a sailor of such caliber at the wheel, whether they could see him or not.

The Great Eastern

On May 1, 1854, Messrs. Scott, Russell, and Company of Millwall, London laid down the keel of Isambard Kingdom Brunel's dream. The six hundred and ninety-two foot ship, weighing in at eighteen thousand, nine hundred and fifteen tons, became the largest ship ever built in its time—four times larger than any other ship. She had a fifty-six foot paddle wheel driven by four steam engines, a twenty-four foot prop driven by one engine, and six masts that could hold eighteen thousand and one hundred forty-eight square feet of sail. The ship was so fast that the sails could not be used in conjunction with the steam engines. It could carry four thousand passengers and held a crew of four hundred and eighteen. The great vessel also carried along a ghost.

She was first called the *S. S. Leviathan*. She was so big; she had to be launched sideways. Multitudes gathered on November 7, 1857 to witness this spectacular event. The ship moved about three feet then stopped. During the launch, a cable snapped and the incident killed two workers. It took three months to push the ship into the sea. The costs were over the top and the Eastern Steam Navigation Company went bankrupt. There she sat, unfinished for a year before the Great Eastern Ship Company bought her and completed the construction of the vessel. They then named it the *Great Eastern*.

She had already been labeled as an unlucky ship. Brunel came on deck while she was being readied for her first test run. As he wandered around, he heard that one of the riveters was missing, and they feared he might have been accidentally sealed into the double iron safety hull. Crewmen were already stirring about the banging noises coming from below and the faint voices heard deep within the bowers of the unlucky ship. A complete search of the vessel produced no evidence of such accusations and plans continued as scheduled. Brunel stopped to have his picture taken on the deck but collapsed moments after. He had suffered a stroke onboard the ship.

A week later, the *Great Eastern* set out on a test run. A boiler overheated in one of the front engine compartments and exploded, sending one of the funnels up like a rocket into the sky. Seven crewmembers were killed in the incident. One was on deck, five others were part of the boiler crew, and one man was killed by the paddle wheel when he dove overboard. Four days later, Brunel died. It is said that the news of this disaster was more than he could stand. The ship was truly cursed.

Her maiden voyage on June 17, 1860, carried but thirty-five passengers. A far cry from the four thousand she could hold. Her size did not stop her from the rolling prone to smaller ships, and many of the passengers were ill for most of the voyage to America. The crew also fought amongst each other and there was much dissention among them. They could not stop hearing the banging of a sharp object against the hull. It would echo throughout the ship at all hours of the night and day.

The thirty-five passengers and four hundred and eighteen-person crew arrived in New York with much fanfare. The expecting throng scattered in a terrified state when the enormous ship tore open the minuscule wharf during landing. It is reported that another person was killed during this incident. The company was losing money fast and could not pay their bills when it was time to leave port. The *Great Eastern* left with one hundred people aboard en route to Halifax, Nova Scotia, then England. In Halifax, the governor imposed a lighthouse fee of seventeen hundred dollars on the ship. This was considered outrageous and the ship turned sail for England without rest. Because of this, an engine screw shaft collapsed and the "monster of the sea" limped into the English port. She was now responsible for over twenty deaths. Countless reports by crew and passengers flowed in to the public of how they had seen and heard the ghost of the missing riveter on the ship.

On her second voyage, she met with a hurricane, and once again, limped into port at New York. This time, the Civil War was taking the country and she was soon hired to transport troops. This was a one-time affair as crewmembers mutinied and were forced into the rigging by the soldiers until surrendering. The sounds of the banging were still persisting, only louder.

On the next cruise, a hurricane overcame her again as she sailed along the Ireland coast. Many of the eight hundred and thirty-two passengers were seriously injured as the ship tossed from side to side. When the rudder broke, all seemed hopeless. A man aboard the ship named Hamilton Towle quickly designed a repair and instituted it, thus saving all aboard. Once in New York, he was given a medal for his bravery but sued the shipping company for their lack of gratitude. He won one hundred thousand dollars of salvage compensation for saving the ship from destruction. On August 27, 1862, the ship sailed out of New York into a heavy gale. The captain turned back towards New York. As he was being piloted back into the harbor, the ship hit bottom. The collision tore a nine-foot wide by eighty-three foot long gash in the outer hull. The inner hull was secure so she sailed into port with no harm to passengers or crew.

Helmet diver, Peter Falcon inspected the damage. Because the ship was too large to dry dock, a series of cofferdams were built around the ship. This consisted of iron plates that would keep the water away from the hull while riveters repaired the ship. While Falcon was inspecting the damage, he frantically pulled on the emergency cord and was quickly hauled up. He ranted that he had heard the ghost of the old riveter hammering while down there. At that point, many of the riveters refused to continue their jobs. Famous New York spiritualist, Seth Thomas was summoned in to rid the ship of its ghost. Instead, he fled the scene with grim news that the spirit will not leave the ship, as his body and spirit are trapped inside. Captain Walter Paton of the *Great Eastern* decided to put to rest the nonsense of ghosts and dove below the water himself. He too, came to the surface a believer. Other men heard the spectral hammering of the hull but a search inside the ship revealed nothing out of the ordinary. The *Great Eastern* sat for one week untouched until only the bravest of riveters came back to complete the job. In December, she was finally ready to sail once more.

The talk of ghosts brought twelve hundred passengers aboard the vessel bound for England. This could not save the investors of the great vessel, and she was converted into a cable-laying ship on April 4, 1864. She was to lay the second transatlantic cable, as the first had broken a year before. The trip was almost a success as the second cable, almost laid, snapped. They went back and tried a third time with success. They were even able to pull the second cable up and take it back. After that she was pretty much outdated and old.

The French bought her and made another voyage. It was on this voyage that two literary greats supposedly met. Jules Verne was aboard the *Great Eastern* when American, North River, New York boat pilot, Herman Melville boarded it. The meeting was of little consequence at the time, but history puts it as a tremendous and strange encounter, as both wrote about great monsters of the sea. Whether they heard the phantom banging or not, is unknown. The spectral hammering was still reported by others.

In 1872, she docked in Liverpool where she stayed until she was bought twelve years later for a sum of twenty-six thousand pounds. She then became a floating billboard before being sold for scrap in 1889, for the sum of 16,000 sixteen thousand pounds. At Rock Ferry, on the River Mersey, she was dismantled. It took eighteen months. All the while the scrappers hammers were matched by the ethereal rapping of another, echoing through the empty hull while they toiled. While the port section was being torn open, an unearthly shriek flooded the vast iron carcass. Workers from below came up shaking and numb with fear. One of them had opened a section of the hull, and there, holding a hammer, was the skeleton of the missing riveter.

Could his spirit have been the cause of all the dreadful incidents that plagued the ship? Was it cursed from the start as being a monster too big for the times? Perhaps a little of both can be blamed for the many disasters that overshadowed the visions of its investors and cut short the lives of many more, starting from the time of its construction, when one man became an eternal and ethereal part of the cursed vessel.

Sam Bellamy and "Goody" Hallett

The story of the pirate Sam Bellamy is well known. His ship, the *Whydah* is labeled as the only pirate wreck ever discovered. Hundreds of thousands of artifacts have been recovered from the wreck off of Wellfleet, Massachusetts. It is blamed on a storm, but some say that a woman's vengeance played a part in his early demise. The *Whydah* has not only imparted a vast treasure in coins and jewels, but has also provided a timeless wealth of knowledge into the daily life of a pirate. It has served to fill many holes that remain perforated in history.

One such discovery was in 2006. Divers found a stocking, fibula, and small shoe at the *Whydah* wreck. They knew it was from a person of small stature. What they later found out was that it was actually from an eleven-year-old boy. Both forensic and court data proved their find. The boy, John King, was with his mother in the Caribbean when Bellamy took their ship and cargo. According to records, it was November 9, 1716, when Bellamy boarded the *Bonetta* and plundered its cargo. Bellamy was with the boat for fifteen days. At that time, John King demanded that he join the piratical crew or he would kill himself. Bellamy, probably admiring the boy's spirit let him aboard. Experts claim that the young were mostly "powder monkeys" who would haul gunpowder from the magazine to the cannons. Records show that King was the youngest known pirate in history.

Many times treasures of knowledge far outweigh those that shine bright in a cache.

It is also known that Sam Bellamy left his wife and family in Canterbury to seek sunken treasure off the coast of Florida. He acquired a sloop in 1716, and sailed for the colonies in search of fortune. He landed in Eastham Harbor on Cape Cod. There, things took an unexpected turn. He met a beautiful fifteen-year-old young woman named Maria Hallett. A romance ensued. He made a promise to her that he would return with a ship full of treasures and they would forever be rich in wealth and love. With that, Sam Bellamy sailed south to find his wealth in lost gold and silver.

Bellamy and a friend who helped fund the expedition, Paulsgrave Williams of Newport, did not exactly find their wealth in the water. In fact, the mission was a total failure. It then dawned on them that better opportunities sat above the waves. From that moment on, they decided to join a privateer. The two joined Benjamin Hornigold's crew of privateers. Hornigold was also the captain who gave us the likes of Blackbeard.

Back in Eastham, Maria Hallett was having Bellamy's child. The town was up in arms over the fact that the young girl was having a baby out of wedlock and to a rover, no less. The baby was born but died shortly after. One account states that it swallowed a piece of straw while Maria hid in a barn to elude authorities. When the townsfolk heard this, they had the officials throw her in jail. She was proclaimed a witch and was soon banished from Eastham forever.

Meanwhile, Bellamy and the crew were not pleased with Captain Hornigold's agenda to attack only French and Spanish vessels. They voted the captain out, putting Bellamy in his place. Williams became quartermaster. This was the beginning of Sam Bellamy's piratical career. In early 1717, Bellamy and Williams had gained command of their own ships. They both spied a ship loaded with ivory along with thousands of silver and gold coins. They pursued the ship for three days before overtaking it. Bellamy was so proud of his plunder that he decided to keep it as his flagship. He transferred the captured crew to his old boat, the *Sultana* and sailed off in the *Whydah*. This was after transferring his other treasures aboard the English galley.

He now had enough treasure and means to return to New England and settle. He began his trek up the East Coast towards New England, taking more prizes along the way. Paulsgrave Williams followed in his sloop but fell behind the much faster *Whydah*. In the meantime, Maria, now a common poor woman known as "Goody," was living in a shack along the beaches of Wellfleet. There she waited each day for the return of her love. Goody was a colonial term given to housewives of modest class stature.

The story takes two turns here. One version is that Maria, heartbroken over her love's supposed betrayal, curses him to suffer eternal unrest. She has been shunned by her people, and is sunken and aged beyond her years. Time, though short in span had taken its toll on the beautiful young woman. Withered and pale, her once graceful gait now resembled that of an old hag. On April 26, 1717, Goody Hallett stood on the beach waiting out the tempest that raged along the cape. The *Whydah* suddenly came into view. She watched in anger and delight as the ship, weighed down with treasure and cannons, struck a sand bar and reeled on its side. The cracking of the hull was almost deafening among the wind and waves. The *Whydah* wrecked fifteen hundred feet from shore. Only two men survived. One was a Cape Cod Indian by the name of John Julian. The other was a Welsh carpenter named Tom Davis. The man they came to know as "Black Bellamy" forced both of them into piracy. Bellamy went down with the ship. The final echoes of Goody Hallett's shrieks of vengeance could be heard among the screams and cries of the men aboard the *Whydah*.

The second version states that Maria Hallett awaited her love's return and was excited to find out he was close by. Then came the storm. Despite the furious winds and wet, she watched for her captain's return. There she spied the *Whydah* through the storm. The ship hit a sandbar only fifteen hundred feet from her terrified eyes and broke apart in front of her. Maria Hallett watched her lover go down at sea. She never married and died heartbroken.

Either story you choose to believe has the same conclusion. Maria Hallett's ghost still roams the dunes of Wellfleet to this day. Some say she is not alone. There is the wraith of a tall dark man wandering the beaches as well. It is that of Sam Bellamy? He is said to roam the area where his treasure lay. Perhaps still guarding what is left of his sunken horde. Some witnesses have reported two opaque figures walking among the sands before vanishing into the midnight air. Could those figures be Bellamy and Goody Hallett? If the first version is true, then perhaps they have reconciled for a long eternity together. If the second version holds more accountability, then they have finally been reunited, strolling along the waters that kept them so close at heart, yet so far away in those final moments of the pirate's fate.

The Mystery of the Carroll A. Deering

One of the greatest mysteries surrounding the disappearance of a crew has kept paranormal researchers on their toes since 1921. The strange accounts of the *Carroll A. Deering* are to this day, unexplained.

The *Carroll A. Deering* was built and launched in Bathe, Maine by the G. G. Deering Company in 1919. She was a mammoth, five-mast schooner designed for commercial transport. She was named after G. G. Deering's son. In August of 1920, the ship prepared to sail from Norfolk, Virginia, with a cargo of coal bound for Rio de Janeiro. William Merritt was her captain and his son S. E. Merritt, had the job of first mate. The majority of the crew consisted of Danish sailors.

Shortly after departure, Captain Merritt became gravely ill. The ship was forced to port in Lewes, Delaware, where the captain relinquished his duty. His son also left the ship to tend to his father. G. G. Deering sent Captain Willis B. Wormell from Lubec, Maine to command the ship. Charles B. McClellan was given the post of first mate. Wormell was a thorough and tidy individual. He was a captain who preferred strict order on his ship. He took a sharp disliking to McClellan from the start.

On September 8, 1920, the *Deering* continued on its journey. The rest of the voyage was uneventful and the cargo unloaded. The captain and crew took liberty while at port. Captain Wormell met his friend, Captain Goodwin. The two had a very interesting talk that would later become questionable evidence in the events that were to follow. He confided in Goodwin that he did not like his crew, least of all, the first mate. The only person onboard he could trust was the engineer, Herbert Bates. After a bit of shore leave, the *Deering* left port on December 2, 1920 for her home in Portland, Maine.

They made a brief stop in Barbados for supplies and liberties but McClellan got inebriated and locked up. Wormell was able to bail him out of jail. An argument ensued and witnesses heard the angry first mate threaten the captain's life. By January 9, 1921, they were able to set sail for home again. The next known sighting of the schooner was by keeper Thomas Jacobson of the Cape Lookout Lightship in North Carolina.

This is where everything becomes a bit strange. Jacobson was hailed by a voice on deck of a crewman who was standing on the quarterdeck. In fact, the whole crew seemed to be congregated in the sacred spot on the ship designated for the captain only. The man was not dressed in official uniform, nor did he speak or act in the manner analogous to that of a commander. He was rather tall with reddish hair. He shouted to Jacobson that the ship had lost its anchors in a gale south of Cape Fear, and to alert the Deering Company. With that the *Carroll A. Deering* sailed out of sight.

The lightship radio was not working at the time. A steamer ominously passed shortly afterward. Jacobson blew the whistle of the lightship. This requires any ships in the area to respond. The steamer did not respond.

The vessel had no visible name on it anywhere. It silently continued on its way.

At eight-thirty a.m. on January 31, 1921, the *Deering* was found grounded on the Diamond Shoals of Cape Hatteras. Her sails were set and her lifeboats were missing. Rescue ships tried in vain to reach the wrecked ship but the breakers were too dangerous. The next day, the Coast Guard Cutter, *Seminole* tried to board the *Deering* but the harsh surf would not allow the boat to get close enough. Both days they noticed there was no crew aboard the ship. She was, to their knowledge, abandoned. Finally, on February 4, 1921, the *Manning* arrived and at ten-thirty a.m., boarded the *Carroll A. Deering*.

The ship was in perfect shape inside. All articles of the officers and crew were missing. The ship's papers, chronometer, log, and navigational instruments were also gone. The rescue crew noticed there was food soaking for the next day's meals. They also noticed that there were three different pairs of boots in the captain's quarters as if three different tenants had bunked there. A large map hung from the wall, marked with the ship's movements at sea. Up until January 23rd, Wormell's unique handwriting graced the chart. After that there was an entirely different script. Once on deck, the men noticed makeshift anchors and red lights running up the main mast indicating that the ship was derelict. They investigated and searched for clues until four-thirty p.m. From there, they left the *Deering*, more perplexed than when they boarded her.

The ship could not be salvaged, and attempts to bring it to port failed. On March 4, 1921, the *Carroll A. Deering* was mined to prevent her from becoming a navigational hazard. This was far from the end of the story. Five different United States government departments investigated the case. About the same time, nine other ships were reported missing in the general area. The *S. S. Hewitt,* with a crew of forty-two men and Captain Hans Jacob Hanson had also disappeared on a course from Sabine, Texas to Portland, Maine. She was very close to the *Deering* at the time of her disappearance.

Some of the theories put forth in their vanishing were:

> 1.) modern pirates,
> 2.) Russian plots to capture American ships and bring then to Russia,
> 3.) rumrunners, perhaps aboard the mystery steamer,
> 4.) something supernatural, and
> 5.) mutiny.

Seven of the ships were later reported lost to a vicious storm that took place off the Atlantic coast. The *Deering* and the *Hewitt,* however, were sailing away from that storm. If the others were accounted for, what happened to the *Hewitt* and the *Deering?*

Authorities thought they had their answer on April 21, 1921, when a man named Christopher Columbus Gray appeared at their door with a message in a bottle. He claimed to have found it on Buxton Beach in North Carolina. The note read,

> "DEERING CAPTURED BY OIL BURNING BOAT SOMETHING LIKE CHASER. TAKING OFF EVERY-THING HANCUFFING CREW. CREW HIDING ALL OVER SHIP. NO CHANCE TO MAKE ESCAPE FINDER PLEASE NOTIFY HEADQUARTERS DEERING."

This appeared to be quite a find. The validity of the bottle and note were checked. The bottle was made in Rio de Janeiro. The handwriting closely matched that of Herbert Bates, Captain Wormell's only trusted crewmember. Still, something was not right. It came to a head when Mr. Gray inadvertently confessed to writing the letter himself. He ran when the authorities came to fetch him but was later apprehended. The reason he wrote the note, he wanted a job as light keeper and thought such a find would make him a hero in the eyes of the government. The government had always thought mutiny might have been the prime explanation for the demise of the crew and ship.

They theorized that McClellan may have killed the captain and kept others prisoner below deck. That would account for three separate pairs of boots in the captain's quarters. The man seen on the quarterdeck that day was Johan Fredrickson. He was the Bos'n. The Bos'n is next in charge after the first mate. Perhaps they tried to escape the ship after mutiny or maybe the captain, first mate, and engineer were killed in a scuffle and the crew, knowing no one would believe them, soon took leave of the ship. According to the chart on the wall, it took six days for them to sail eighty miles.

Why would someone take so long to go such a short distance unless they were trying to figure out their next move? There are countless questions that remain unanswered in the accounts and whereabouts of the crew of the *Carroll A. Deering*. Paranormal researchers, to this day, peruse endless writings of the investigations and records of the ships movements from the time of its building to its last moments where the truth went down with the ship. No lifeboats were ever recovered nor were any of the crew.

One strange fact came out of Portland, Oregon. A Cyril A. McClellan was issued a seaman's certificate on March 20, 1921. The Department of Justice went into action and found that the address he had given when obtaining the license was actually the Sailor's Union Office of Portland, Oregon. They also found that no one by that name had shipped out of any ports or vessels whatsoever. There were no records of a Cyril A. McClellan ever existing before the certificate was issued and the person was never seen or heard from again.

The sighting of the men on the quarterdeck, the chart with the other handwriting, the missing logs and navigational equipment, and most of all, the missing crew—what really did happen to the *Carroll A. Deering* in January of 1921? The answer lies far away in time, yet forever in eternity.

Conclusion

Many of these accounts have been handed down through history. Some are just as history tells them. Some may have been diluted, while others have suffered the acts of poetic license to the point where truth has been lost to antiquity. Folklore, though a wonderful part of history can tend to overshadow the actual accounts. Presented within this book are the stories as best as history will provide. Facts and folklore are inevitably blended together in some cases. The others are as they are, all accounted in history. Any places that change during the time of this writing and its publication are just due to the passing of time and progress.

Appendix A
Types of Ships Mentioned

Bark (Barque)
Bark is the American spelling of a ship that has three or more masts. The aftermost mast is the only one that is fore-and-aft rigged.

Brig
This is a two-mast vessel whose sails are square-rigged much like the Mayflower.

Brigantine
A two-mast ship. The foremost mast is square-rigged but the main mast is fore-and-aft rigged. It is kind of a mixture between a bark and brig.

Clipper
A multi-mast ship designed for speed. They had a lot of sails and were meticulously designed to move quickly over the water. Merchants used these to out-run privateers and pirates, although the latter had them as well.

Cutter
A small fore-and-aft rigged single-mast boat with two or more headsails and a bowsprit. Although a cutter and a sloop are similar, the difference is that the cutter's mast is further towards the stern as opposed to the sloop.

Galleon

This is a multi-decked sixteenth century warship. It still saw use through the seventeenth century but was replaced by the faster designs of the times. The galleon was primarily used as a warship as noted by the many cannons usually on board.

Galley

A warship with a single sail but mainly powered by oars.

Man of war

The term for a giant warship. They were outfitted with many cannons and were designed primarily to fight.

Schooner

This is a fore-and-aft rigged vessel where the foremast is shorter than the other masts.

Shallop

A large sixteenth century vessel that is fore-and-aft rigged. Shallops were generally bulky and carried much cargo.

Sloop

A fore-and-aft rigged vessel. The single mast is further forward than that of a cutter. Therefore, the fore-triangle sail is also smaller than ones found on a cutter.

Appendix B
A Timeline of Notable
Pirates Mentioned

1619-1671—Phillip Babb
Babb was reported to have been a pirate. Perhaps he was one of the many who aided the corsairs when they visited the Isles of Shoals. Either way, he was born in 1619, and died March 31, 1671. He is buried in the Babb burial ground on the isles. Whether he was an actual pirate or not is a matter of conjecture.

1689-1701—Captain William Kidd
Captain Kidd roamed the seas as a privateer turned pirate until his arrest and hanging at Execution Dock on May 5, 1701.

1703-1704—John (Jack) Quelch
Quelch is said to be the first to fly the "Jolly Roger." His career, like many other freebooters, was short. He was hung in 1704.

1713?-1718—Blackbeard (Edward Teach or Thatch)
He first worked as a privateer. He hooked up with Captain Benjamin Hornigold and was later given command of his own ship. His piratical career spanned twenty-seven months until Captain Maynard brought him to justice on November 22, 1718.

1714-1718—Sandy Gordon

Gordon became a pirate after he mutinied aboard the *Porpoise* and took the captain's daughter, Martha Herring, as his wife. He later joined forces with Blackbeard. He was given his own ship, the *Flying Scot* to command. Gordon and the *Flying Scot* met their end off the Isles of Shoals in 1718.

Black Bartelmy

It is unclear if this pirate is one of fact, fiction, or folklore. There are fictional tales of his name. This is one the reader will enjoy puzzling out for himself or herself.

1716-1717—Sam Bellamy

Black Bellamy came to the American coast in search of buried treasure but found a more lucrative trade in robbing ships. His career was cut short by a storm off of Cape Cod where he perished with his ship the *Whydah* on April 26, 1717.

1717-1718—Stede Bonnet

A well respected Major of middle age decided to become a pirate. He was a gentleman pirate but that did not save him from the noose in December of 1718.

1719-1722—Bartholomew Roberts

Black Bart was a fancy dresser during battle. He admired bravery in his enemy and often rewarded them for such an attribute. He met his end on February 10, 1722, when grapeshot fired from a cannon aboard the *H.M.S. Swallow* hit him in the throat.

1719?-1720—Anne Bonney

Anne Bonney joined up with "Calico" Jack Rackham in a short stint of piracy. Along with them was Mary Read. The three were captured and Calico Jack was hung in 1720. Anne and Mary were pregnant and therefore were granted temporary reprieve. Mary died in prison shortly after childbirth. Anne was never hanged. Her end is uncertain. It is reported that her father may have paid a ransom for her release. There are accounts that she lived into her eighties. This sounds like another mystery for the reader to follow up on.

1722-1723/4?—Ned Lowe (Low)

He was a brutal pirate with a very short career spanning fourteen months. There are two stories regarding his demise. The first one states that he was last seen in 1723 around the canaries and Azores. After that, his ship disappeared forever, presumably lost to a storm. The other tells that the crew actually mutinied and sent him overboard in a small boat with no provisions. A French vessel rescued him two days later. Someone recognized him as the wicked pirate. He was speedily tried and hanged in 1724.

Bibliography

Botkin, B.A. *A Treasury of New England Folklore*. New York: Bonanza Books, 1947.

Cahill, Robert Ellis. *Ghostly Haunts*. Peabody, MA: Chandler Smith Publishing House, 1983.

Cahill, Robert Ellis. *Pirates and Lost Treasures*. Salem, MA: Old Saltbox Publishing, (date unknown).

Cahill, Robert Ellis. *Things That Go Bump in the Night*. Peabody, MA: Chandler-Smith Publishing House, 1989.

D'Agostino, Thomas. *Haunted Rhode Island*. Atglen PA: Schiffer Publishing Limited, 2005.

D'Agostino, Thomas. *Haunted New Hampshire*. Atglen, PA: Schiffer Publishing Limited, 2006.

D'Agostino, Thomas. *Haunted Massachusetts*. Atglen, PA: Schiffer Publishing Limited, 2006.

Drake, Samuel Adams. *A Book of New England Legends and Folklore in Prose and Poetry*. Boston, MA: Little, Brown, and Company, 1883.

Middleton, Richard Barnham. *The Ghost Ship and Other Stories*. New York: Mitchell, Kennedy, Cloth, 1912.

Oppel, Frank. *Tales of New England Past*. Secaucus, NJ: Castle, 1987.

Rutledge, Lyman V. *The Isles of Shoals in Lore and Legend*. Barre, MA: Barre Publishers, 1965.

Skinner, Charles Montgomery. *Myths and Legends of Our Land*. Philadelphia and London: J.B. Lippencott Company, 1896.

Smitten, Susan. *Ghost Stories of New England*. Auburn, WA: Ghost House Books, 2003.

Snow, Edward Rowe. *Pirates and Buccaneers of the Atlantic Coast*. Boston, MA: Yankee Publishing, 1944.

Snow, Edward Rowe. *Ghosts, Gales, and Gold*. New York: Dodd, Mead, and Company, 1972.

Thompson, William O. *Coastal Ghosts and lighthouse Lore*. Kennebunk, ME: "Scapes Me", 2001.

Verde, Thomas A. *Maine Ghosts and Legends*. Camden, ME: Down East Books, 1989.

Index